I WENT TO BAPTIST KID'S CAMP

&

CAME HOME SPEAKING IN TONGUES

A HOLY GHOST STORY

JUDY MCKENZIE MCCLARY

Magnolia Publications

I Went to Baptist Kid's Camp & Came Home Speaking in Tongues: *A Holy Ghost Story*
Judy McKenzie McClary

Published by Magnolia Publications

Unless otherwise noted, all Scripture quotations are from the New King James Version of the Bible. Copyright © 1979, 1980, 1982 by Thomas Nelson, Inc., publishers. Used by permission.

Scripture quotations marked AMP are from the Amplified Bible. Old Testament copyright © 1965, 1987 by the Zondervan Corporation. The Amplified New Testament copyright © 1954, 1958, 1987 by the Lockman Foundation. Used by permission.

Scripture quotations marked NIV are from the Holy Bible, New International Version of the Bible. Copyright © 1973, 1978, 1984, International Bible Society. Used by permission.

Scripture quotations marked NLT are taken from the Holy Bible, New Living Translation, copyright © 1996, 2004, 2007 by Tyndale House Foundation. Used by permission of Tyndale House Publishers, Inc., Carol Stream, Illinois 60188. All rights reserved.

International Standard Book Number: 978-0-9747292-0-6
Available from Amazon.com and other retail outlets.

This book is lovingly dedicated to my husband,
Charles, who has consistently given me support and
encouragement as I researched and wrote on the
essential issue of baptism and the Church.

CONTENTS

Acknowledgments

My thanks to my husband, Charles, and our children and grandchildren for dinner table discussions and always being there for me; also to our Presbyterian pastor Rev. Paul G. Waite and his wife who guided our family during the first twenty years of our journey into the Christian life. Thanks also to Rosemary, my first-ever Bible teacher and to Bonnie, a friend from the study, who took our family under her wing and through numerous invitations to Spirit-filled sermons and Sunday dinners imparted to us a picture of godly Christian living. Thanks also to Rev. G. Mark Denyes, Pentecostal pastor, who answered questions and patiently advised me as I began to study the theology of the Spirit. And last but not least, I wish to thank the seven-member prayer group who came alongside me as I began to research and write about the Bible and Church history: Diane, Mary Lynn, Arlene, Sharon, Dodie, Donna, and Alice.

PART I

THE BEGINNING

1

Theology Not Spoken at our House

When I was growing up, theological terms were not spoken at our house. I don't think my father understood much about God and salvation even though he had a greater education than his ten older brothers and sisters. My mother had been raised in the Lutheran church and, as I found out later, had very much wanted her children to know Bible stories and pray before meals.

I say all this to say that, to my knowledge, religion was never mentioned at our house; that is, until one day when a newish car pulled in and drove up our long driveway to the house. My dad was working in the yard and he went over to the rolled down window of the car (as people did in those days). At least, that's what rural people did.

It happened to be my oldest sister's friend, Lois. Lois was twenty-something and she asked my dad if it was okay if she and her parents stopped by on Sunday mornings and took some of us thirteen children to Sunday school and church. It took Lois a lot of convincing to get my dad to say yes. This was

3

because Lois and her family were Baptists and they were frowned upon by my Presbyterian father, even though he and his family of origin had never attended the little white Presbyterian church with the high steeple in our neighboring town.

In due time, under the influence of the energetic and loud preaching of the Baptist minister, my older sister made a decision to follow Christ. She came home excited and asked my dad if she could be baptized in water to show Jesus that she really believed. My dad refused and her fervency died down. Being baptized was never brought up in our house again because that was not the way our Presbyterian church did it.

Meanwhile, summer was approaching and there was talk of Bible camp in all our Sunday morning classes. I had no understanding of what happened at a Bible camp and so did not have a particular desire to go. Either that, or the fact that our large family had no extra money to put out for anything that was not entirely necessary, might have been the reason that I never entertained any illusions about going to camp.

All that was to change! Unexpectedly one warm midsummer morning, the neighbor's car pulled into our driveway and Lois got out. I had a bird's eye view because I had been sent up the hill earlier in the morning to hoe carrots in our large garden. I was a curious 12-year old and had gone down to see what the visit was about but was soon sent back to work while she and my dad talked. I was down by the house long enough to figure out that it was me they were talking about.

Lois had stopped by our house to see if my parents would allow her to take me to Bible camp with her and at least one other girl named Betty who I knew was already planning to go. Lois wanted to take me, too, but my dad was not interested in sending me. He said it cost too much. Lois said the church was willing to 'scholarship' me. My dad did not want to take charity as he put it. Lois said they 'scholar-shipped' lots of kids, but still my dad said "no."

I returned to the garden to hoe and keep an eye on the proceedings. I could see Lois excitedly telling him something. Then I could see his slower response. This went on for what seemed like hours but probably wasn't that long. Suddenly I very much wanted to go to camp, whatever that was. While they discussed whether or not this was going to happen, I realized that it maybe was in the realm of possibility. I remember that I prayed (I don't recall praying before that time); I said, "Oh, Lord, please let me go. I promise to not have any fun and to study my Bible every minute."

Dumb prayer of a twelve-year old. Actually, I remember one other time that I prayed. That one got answered, too. It was a cold winter and we were almost out of firewood to heat the house. I was maybe ten or eleven and my dad had taken me, my next-in-age sister and our younger brother along to help cut wood. We drove what seemed like a very long way to cut wood before the cavernous stove in our living room burned up its meager supply.

We had to go deep into the woods. It was a terrible day; that winter was so cold and we lurched along in our old truck that didn't have a heater. None of us kids complained. We knew how important it was to get back with firewood. We arrived at a place where I could tell my father had cut wood before.

We kids tried to keep warm as we took turns helping my dad run the old chain saw and carrying the chunks that had been cut into the back of the truck. Suddenly the chainsaw slipped and cut my dad on the shin of his leg. I could tell it was bad because there was a straight-across tear in his pant leg and blood was pouring out.

Even at ten or eleven, I knew that time was of the essence. We were deep in the woods and no one would be coming to look for us. My mother didn't drive and we had only the one vehicle anyway. My dad was losing blood fast. We hurried back to where we'd left the truck, leaving a red trail of blood behind us. My dad was limping and carrying the big saw. We got into the truck and the truck would not start. He tried over and over again. It was no use. And the blood kept flowing. He got out of the truck and just wept.

I had never seen my father cry before and I didn't want to look at him. I took my younger brother and sister and we went a little ways away. Holding hands, we did something the three of us had never done before and never did after. I prayed something like this: "Dear God. Please start the truck and get us home safely so my mother can bandage my dad's leg." I don't know if I knew enough to say "Amen" or not.

To this day, I don't know how I knew enough to pray but when we got back to the truck, it started and the blood had stopped flowing out of my dad's leg. We were shivering in the cold and my dad backed the truck around until we could get out of that woods and back home. When my mother lifted his pant leg and saw the gaping wound she gasped. She bandaged the hole shut and said she was amazed that my dad had not bled to death out there in the woods. That was my only other prayer.

Bible camp was to start that afternoon and Lois stayed talking to my dad for what seemed like hours. He finally gave in and said I could go. I was excited and I forgot all about my plan not to have any fun. I had lots of fun. I had never really had a chance to play in a lake before and it was glorious. There was a cute boy in my class and they had chapel every night and there for the first time that I was aware of, I heard what they were saying about God.

Others from my cabin were making decisions to follow Christ. I didn't know what that meant so I listened closely. And a thought kept coming to me: This may be your last chance to accept Christ. Where will you spend eternity? In heaven or in hell? Where? Where? Where? Echoed through my head all week. The words were actually from a song that was played every night after the evangelist finished giving his message. The words stuck with me all day. It didn't matter if we were swimming or goofing off with our camp counselor or doing crafts, I couldn't get away from those words.

Added to that was the thought in my head, "This

may be your last chance to accept Me." I was miserable. Finally on the last night before our week was over and we were to leave for home the next day, I made up my mind—I was going forward to give my life to Christ. Just as I finally got up my courage, the music stopped. Camp was over.

I slipped out the side door of the little tabernacle. I was devastated. I was so disappointed. Another girl from my cabin had gone down in front and made a public confession for Jesus. She was so happy and was crying and blubbering for joy. Everybody was congratulating her. I turned and went out the side door and headed for the woods. I wanted to be alone as I walked back to my cabin. To my surprise the same thought came back even more insistently: This may be your last chance. Do you want to accept Me now?" I knew it was Jesus and I said a heartfelt "Yes!"

Immediately I could feel that I was born again even though I didn't have the theology to put it into words. It was like the happiest feeling inside. In the days and weeks to come, I could sing in a funny little language that wasn't English and which I now know the Bibles calls 'tongues.' I didn't know then that it was supposed to be a part of the package of God for new believers. Later I would discover the Scripture that explained my experience: "…repent, and let every one of you be baptized into the name of Jesus for the remission of sins; and you will receive the gift of the Holy Spirit." (Acts 2:38, 39)

So although I had no understanding of what had happened theologically, I knew inside it was right and I was overjoyed. I walked back to my cabin ahead of everybody else; climbed up to the top bunk, and reveled in the goodness of God. I was a happy, happy 12-year old who went to sleep that night knowing that all was well with my soul.

True to the words I had heard, it had been my last chance to hear the gospel. On the drive home, I didn't say anything to Lois who had brought me. Indeed, I would not have had the words to tell her what had happened inside. I just rode along silently, as was my want, but when I got home; I immediately started telling my younger brother and sister that I had gotten 'saved.'

When my dad heard that, he immediately took us out of the church. It was truly my last chance to hear the gospel. He told Lois and her family that none of us kids would be going to their church again, that we were going to our own church. We didn't, but it was too late—what I already had in my heart could not be taken from me and even though I did not understand being 'born again' or the Holy Spirit, I always had that comforting presence with me—I just didn't know why.

So fast forward twenty years. I was ready to run my Christian race. I had started attending Rosemary's neighborhood Bible study and week-after-week pearls dropped from her lips as she taught us the Word of God. Bonnie, a Pentecostal lady at the study, probably seeing my absolute ignorance of spiritual things, took me under her wing and taught me day-by-day things about Jesus Christ. She loved the Bible and taught me to love it, too.

I still hadn't been baptized in water but I wanted to be. You know, submerged, like it says in the Bible (Acts 2:38-39). It was a driving force within me. I had been baptized as an infant, but somehow it just didn't seem right to me. I talked to our Presbyterian pastor and he said that if I wanted, the church could rent a room at the Holiday Inn and I could be baptized in their pool. Then we could all swim and have a potluck afterward.

This seemed irreverent to me so I said no. But when he told me we could wait until our Labor Day church campout and be baptized at a nearby lake, I jumped at the chance. Three days before the great event, I wanted to fast. Not knowing exactly how to do it, I stopped all food and water for three days. Then I waited for the pastor to say it was the right time.

It was cold that weekend, colder than other similar Labor Day weekends. Maybe that was why the subject was never brought up. He seemed to have forgotten all about my water baptism and everybody finally packed up. The weekend was over and I remained unbaptized—but I still wanted to be.

I know that God must have had other reasons for not allowing it, but at the time, I was very disappointed. Soon, however, I heard from someone that the Pentecostal church near us was having a water baptism as a part of their church service. This seemed right to me so I called the church office and they signed me up, too.

That night there were several backslidden

teenagers who were being re-baptized to get a new start. They were saying how much they loved Jesus and telling sordid stories one after another and marveling in the fact that Jesus would still take them back. I panicked momentarily. I had not been told that I would need to say something.

Inwardly I prayed, "Lord, what will I say?" Back came His quiet voice in my spirit, but as clear as could be, "Say, 'I come in obedience.'"

When my turn came and I was asked why I wanted to be baptized, I assured them that I, too, loved Jesus but I added, "I come in obedience." Even years later, people would come up to me and say, "I remember your baptism."

And—glory to God—as I came up out of the water, I was enveloped in a new peace.[1] I knew I had done it the way Jesus said.

> And that water is a picture of baptism, which now saves you, *not from removing dirt from your body, but as a response to God from a clean conscience.* It is effective because of the resurrection of Jesus Christ."
> (I Peter 3:21 TLT)

I felt I had finally done everything He told me.[2] All was now right between me and my God.

Chapter 1 Endnotes

---

[1] I Peter 3:21
[2] Acts 2:38-39

2

Growing in Spiritual Things

In all those years, I had no formal Bible teaching—not much more than the camp sermons— so I had no one to tell me that the Holy Spirit wasn't the same today as He was two thousand years ago. I had no clue that there was a word for the funny little language that came to me when I said 'yes' to Jesus.

Actually I remember going to church only one other time after my Baptist Bible camp experience. It was before I was married. The young man who is now my husband and his college friends decided to impress their steadies by taking us to church.

The church was quite fancy. Compared to the little plain Baptist church, it *was very fancy.* The church had some kind of foot rest that pulled out, I think, which some of the people knelt on some of the time. I didn't know when to kneel and when to sit so it kept me quite busy.

It would be years before I would be in church again. At the time I didn't understand that the church was divided up into little pieces called denominations but I don't think it would have made much of an impression on me anyway.

It was now eighteen years since I had received my Bible camp experience. Even so, I didn't even know I had been what is called born-again and I didn't have any knowledge of God or, I must admit, any interest in learning more—I was pretty happy with life just as it was.

Rosemary, a Baptist neighbor lady, had invited me to her Bible study but it was on Tuesday mornings and my daughter had ballet lessons on Tuesdays. Anyway, studying the Bible didn't seem all that interesting to me. Things were about to change!

Those years—the late sixties and early seventies—were years of economic downturn in the aeronautical industry. My husband, an electrical engineer, worked for a large corporation that was beginning to feel its effects. Not wanting to lose quality engineers to layoff, they asked my husband and about a dozen other engineers if they would consider going to Atlanta, Georgia for six to eight weeks to support the flight test program for Lockheed, a company designing a military transport aircraft.

They all said "Yes" because there really wasn't any other choice. This left me alone in Minnesota with a newly-purchased house, a kindergartner and a three-year old. Weeks turned into months. Chuck and the others would fly home to their families every third weekend or so. Because we had just bought our home and because, as far as any of us knew, the men would be home permanently after the next three-week stint, we stayed in Minneapolis. In February, the kids and I joined him for a month and got to see a bit of Georgia.

I stayed busy that year as vice-president of our local PTA in charge of choosing and setting up programs for the monthly meetings. Spring arrived. School let out. I took our children and joined my husband in Atlanta along with the other men's families. My husband was not feeling well that summer so evenings while other families went on sightseeing excursions he went to bed early as did our little ones.

I was left alone. Never having been a TV fan and having no magazines or other entertainment, I turned to the only reading material in our kitchenette—the Gideon Bible. Every morning after getting the kids fed and our husbands off to work, we wives would gather at the pool so our children could swim. They told about the sightseeing their families were doing and asked what I was doing to keep busy. I mentioned that I was reading the Bible and finding some mighty interesting things in it.

After that, every morning I would be asked what I had read the night before. I would entertain them with the past evening's 'juicy' stories that I had read from the Bible. We all loved it but unplanned by me, I was also gaining an understanding of the Bible. It was no longer just 'silly business;' what I was learning was deeply fascinating.

When we all returned home at the end of summer, I no longer had the Gideon Bible that I'd used in Atlanta. It was then that the same Baptist lady who had invited me earlier to her Bible study got wind that we were home again and again invited me to join her group. This time I excitedly said "Yes!"

They were just finishing the Book of John and were about to begin the Book of Acts the following week. Everyone was puzzling over a prayer language that the early Church apparently took for granted.

> Then Peter said to them, 'Repent, and let *every one of you* be baptized in the name of Jesus Christ for the remission of sin; and you shall receive the gift of the Holy Spirit. (Acts 2:38, emphasis added)

Apparently this baptism was to continue until the end of time.

> For the promise is to you and to your children, and to all who are afar off, as many as the Lord will call. (Acts 2:39)

Rosemary and the group were very interested in what this 'gift of the Holy Spirit' was. She said it was some kind of language. This was new territory for her (and certainly for me) even though she had been saved for many years. But being of a spiritual bend and longing to know God better and loving the Word of God as she did, if something was in the Bible, she wanted to know more about it.

I was very much interested, too. Having learned some things that were in the Bible while we were in

Georgia, I now wanted to know more. It was hard to believe there were such fascinating things in the Bible as I was reading. Once I started going, I don't think I missed once.

There was a beautiful, sweet-faced, white-haired old lady named Lillian that always came. She was quiet and kept her opinions to herself. I was to find out later, she was a prayer warrior. Now I know why we got so many prayers answered for our families and so soon! I would later find out that she kept track of our prayer requests and talked to God about us and our problems during the rest of the week. While we were busy visiting with our neighbors and shopping and taking care of our young families that dear woman took our problems into her prayer closet and asked God for help and His mercy on us the rest of the week. She was the steel backbone of that little group.

Although she didn't tell us about herself, I later found out that she knew all about the Holy Spirit. Her father had been a well known evangelist and she had traveled extensively with him and her mother during her early years. Lillian had married a man who became a drunk and lived a tough life, finally praying her husband into sobriety. She did not have much time left on this earth but she was determined to bring all of "her girls" into an understanding of Jesus Christ and the Book of Acts.

Being the newest member of the group, I didn't understand as did the other neighbor ladies the excitement of discovering the early Church's process of initiation into the gift of the Holy Spirit. All took place before I was, at last, baptized in water. It was all new to me. I was just discovering these things as the group asked questions and read from the Bible.

So I was pretty amazed at the study with everyone else talking about being baptized in the Holy Spirit and 'receiving the gift of the Holy Spirit' and what about talking in tongues and who could have it and who couldn't. It was all way above my head. They kept talking about the "Promise of the Father" so I now set out to learn about something called the Promise of the Father and the "baptism" of the Holy Spirit:

> And being assembled together with them, He commanded them not to depart from Jerusalem, but to wait for the promise of the Father, "which," He said, "you have heard from Me; for John truly baptized with water, but you shall be baptized with the Holy Spirit not many days from now."
> (Acts 1:3-4)

One day it dawned on me that the prayer language referred to in the Book of Acts was the very language I had received when I'd had my experience of being born again back behind the tabernacle when I was twelve at the Bible camp. I realized that it was the 'sign' they were talking about. Because I'd had no teaching, I hadn't realized what had happened to me when I said 'yes' to Jesus as a child. Also I had no one telling me the doctrine of the Holy Spirit was old-fashioned or a thing of past centuries.

I hadn't known enough to ask for what I later learned was the 'baptism of the Holy Spirit;' but neither was there anyone telling me I shouldn't. It was part of the package I received that night at Bible camp. It hadn't made a lot of sense to me at the time, but as we studied the Book of Acts I learned that *this was that* in which my neighbors were all so interested—my ears perked up.

And so it was that I discovered that I had already received the *seal* of the Holy Spirit and the *sign* of tongues which my neighbors were just beginning to seek[1].Yet they knew so much more about God than I did. Most of them had been taken to church by their parents as children and they knew all the Bible stories and what to do and not to do in church. They had already been teaching their children. I had never been taken to church and was completely ignorant of the things of the Spirit.

One thing began troubling me now that I was meeting regularly with other Christians. In their seeking, some were discussing all the good and negative things they had heard over the years about speaking in tongues. I began to worry that my unknown language was not genuine—that maybe Satan was trying to fool me with it.

I had not known about all the controversy that flurried around the gifts of the Spirit when I had gotten my prayer language at the age of twelve. I had been all alone in the woods, back of the cabin. Over the years nobody had challenged me when I sang and sang in the Spirit; or when I sang in tongues at home while I was ironing. They didn't know what it was and neither did I. It just sounded good.

This rose to a point of crisis within me after I began studying with other Christians. I started to worry that maybe I was praying something wrong now that I knew others were worried about it. They were all churchgoers who had been taught different opinions about tongues depending upon which denomination they belonged to. God Himself would settle the issue for me a short time later.

Our son was in first grade by now and off to school full days. I had just picked up our daughter from pre-school and we were driving to Northwestern bookstore. The battle over tongues was raging in me as we drove along. Were tongues for today or not? Was I praying something wrong like some worried?

When someone had said 'someone had told them' that tongues were of the devil—was I ever taken aback! As my little girl and I drove along that day, I was wrestling with God. I told Him in no uncertain terms that *I was never ever* going to speak in 'my language' again unless I was positively sure it was from Him. *And I meant it.*

My daughter went on chattering about her little girl activities at pre-school and I was driving along and finding her amusing so I forgot all about my quarrel with God about tongues.

As I listened to her and drove along, I began to hum a little tune under my breath. Soon, without really thinking about it, I started to get some words to the same tune—but they were words in my unlearned language. I was doing it kind of mindlessly as I drove along which one can do once they get used to praying in tongues.

The melody repeated itself and I continued to get different words to the same tune as I sang. This happened maybe three-four times. It was kind of like having a jingle from a commercial that plays in your mind with no effort—or maybe at Christmas time, it might be a familiar carol or some other song that goes through your head. It was quite effortless. Then it stopped.

After a moment or two, it started back up. Not out loud, but it was there in the back of my mind, nevertheless. The music was the same, but now the words I was getting were in English—so I sang them. And they rhymed!

This happened three-four times. They were like a rhyming poem of praise to God. Each time the words were different, but they rhymed—that was important to me because I knew I couldn't have thought up those verses that fast and even made them rhyme.

And so God very kindly showed me my tongues were from Him. I was convinced and to this day, I've remained convinced. I've never doubted from that day to this that my tongues are genuine and come from the Holy Spirit.[2]

Chapter 2 Endnotes

---

[1] I Corinthians 14:22; Mark16:17
[2] Luke 11:12

3

Getting Up to Speed

The Holy Spirit was becoming very real to me. I didn't understand why other people did not have an alive, give-and-take relationship with Him. I knew there was nothing special about me that caused me to have the Holy Spirit with tongues as my prayer language. In fact, the Bible says that God is no respecter of persons.

I knew I had received it in a private manner without other people's opinions influencing me. Later, there was nobody to discourage my using it— and mostly I sang while I was ironing—but because my Dad didn't allow us to attend that little Baptist church anymore, nobody knew it was speaking in tongues and so also nobody had the opportunity to tell me they weren't real.

Eighteen years later when I had started at that little Bible study and they were reading the Book of Acts, we saw that the Holy Spirit was intended to be an aid and a comfort to all believers. I wondered why He was so maligned. Why did people keep trying to prove that He was not for our time or, worse yet, that He was a figment of the imagination?

> However, when He the Spirit of truth has come, He will guide you into all truth; for

> He will not speak on His own authority, but
> whatever He hears He will speak; and He
> will tell you things to come. He will glorify
> Me for He will take of what is Mine and
> declare it to you." (John 15:13-14)

One week our Bible study teacher took us to visit
the pastor of a large, nearby Pentecostal church. He
allowed us to ask any questions we wanted. At that
time, I was quite taken aback by the term, *Holy
Ghost* (as the old King James Bible refers to the Holy
Spirit). As I rode home with one of the neighbor
ladies, I told her she need not pick me up next week,
'that I wasn't getting into anything weird."

That night, my husband went to bed early and our
little ones were already fast asleep. I had nothing to
do as the TV didn't interest me and so I decided to
get out my Bible and read something. By now, my
husband and I had started going to church for the
first time and we had chosen the Presbyterian church
because we had been married in my family's
Presbyterian church.

Someone there told us we needed to get a Bible so
we went to a Christian bookstore and bought what
was called a 'Scofield edition.' It was a large study
Bible and had a huge amount of biblical 'helps' with
notes on everything. I let it fall open where it would
and it fell open to a page that had some paragraphs
about the Holy Spirit and it listed all the references to
the Holy Spirit in the New Testament. That night,
before I went to bed, I looked up every verse listed. I
was amazed! It was more information than I could

ever have imagined but it was good stuff. I knew I would never, never fear the Holy Spirit again, or think He was unknowable.

When one woman said she'd heard that not all were supposed to speak in tongues, it started me on another round of study. I learned she was right! The Bible says there are nine gifts of the Spirit and one of them is *diversities* of tongues. We all get to have a prayer language but 'divers kinds of tongues' means we don't all get the additional tongues that allow one to give a message in church, for example.

> To another the working of miracles; to another prophecy; to another discerning of spi-rits; to another <u>divers kinds of tongues</u>; to another the interpretation of tongues.
> (1Corinthians 12:10 kjv, emphasis added)

Diversities meant 'different kinds' or varieties so there are other kinds of tongues rather than just the one given as a 'sign' when you get born again that you have received the Holy Spirit. So one of the diverse kinds of tongues referred to is a special and unique type of tongues not given to everyone in the whole body of Christ.

For in verse 11 of that same chapter, I found the reason why not everyone has the gift of tongues that allows them to give messages in church (for that is one of the diversities of the gift of tongues—a kind that is only to be used in a church setting). It's because the Holy Spirit doles out different spiritual gifts to different members of the body of Christ. So it is just as the woman had said!

> But one and the same Spirit works all these
> things, distributing to each one individually
> as He will. (I Corinthians 12:11)

By now I had learned another thing about the
diversity of tongues. There are also diverse
languages given by the Spirit! It's kind of fun. After
I'd been praying for quite a while, I prayed and asked
God for a different language than the one I had
initially been given. Then I started to pray in my
prayer language. To my surprise, out came a
different language! I soon asked for my old one back
though, because the new one was more difficult to
enunciate and I wanted to be able to pray fast when I
was in intercession. Again—in midsentence—it
changed back to my old language! I thought that was
amazing.

Because the Holy Spirit is so personable, I tried
to learn everything in the New Testament that I could
find about Him. But I wondered—if there is so much
about the Holy Spirit in the New Testament—what
about the Old Testament? When I heard that a Bible
teacher named Marilyn Hickey was coming to the
nearby Pentecostal church where we had met with
the pastor and that she was going to teach on the
Holy Spirit, I was excited. Would I go? You bet I
would!

There I learned that God had gone to all the
trouble to have His writers include information about
the Holy Spirit in almost every book of the Old
Testament! I was surprised at this. Some people and
some denominations were basically saying He was a

fly-by-night experience—that He had been needed only for a few short years after the birth, death and resurrection of Christ to get the early Church started and then was needed no more because the Bible had already been written.

But I thought God had gone to an awful lot of work to put something in every book of the Old Testament if it was only to be a fleeting experience between mankind and the Holy Spirit. I had already discovered the unlikelihood that God withdrew Him from the Church because I was learning from Ms. Hickey that every book in the Old Testament contained references to the Holy Spirit and besides that, there were also the twenty-seven New Testament books, each one having reference to Him.

First there was discussion about Jesus' experience with the Holy Spirit as He alighted on Him at the River Jordan in the form of a dove; then His explanation to His disciples that He was leaving them but was sending something better—the Holy Spirit. Then Jesus ascended back into heaven and, on the Day of Pentecost, the Holy Spirit arrived with great fanfare and empowered 3,000 new believers!

I decided that the Holy Spirit's presence in the Old Testament was very important for today's Christians to know about for this suggested that the Holy Spirit—or 'the Spirit' as He is referred to in the Old Testament—has always been a very serious part of God's plan for mankind.

4

The Holy Spirit in the Old Testament

I soon discovered the Holy Spirit was just as active in the Old Testament as He is in the New Testament! According to the author of *Systematic Theology: An Introduction to Biblical Doctrine,* "the work of the Holy Spirit is to manifest the active presence of God in the world, and especially in the church."[1]

As I studied how many times the Holy Spirit is written about in both the Old Testament and the New, I was impressed! To me, it seemed unlikely that God would have put all the effort into making sure we knew how important the Spirit was to Him and His people only to have His empowering completely disappear from the Christian life a few short years after Christ's resurrection.

I began to make a list of some of the amazing things done by the Holy Spirit in the Old Testament (as well as the New Testament). He is referred to in many different ways besides "Holy Spirit." For example, He is the "Spirit," or the "Spirit of God" or the "Spirit of the Lord;" but mainly, in the Old Testament, He is simply referred to as "the Spirit."

In the verses below, so that it can be seen that the Holy Spirit is not some johnny-come-lately addition to the New Testament but was equally active with God all throughout the Old Testament, it will be shown that He was a phenomenally important part of God's plan for His people all through the Ages.

> You send forth Your Spirit, they are created;
> and You renew the face of the earth.
> (Psalm 104:30)

Though a pagan, even the Pharaoh of Egypt could recognize the indwelling Spirit of God in Joseph (with the coat of many colors). He saw there was something unique about Joseph—a holiness and a certain wisdom about him—which he rightfully attributed to the God of heaven. As a result, Joseph was made his top administrator in Egypt in charge of the welfare of the whole land:

> And Pharaoh said to his servants, 'Can we find such a one as this, a man in whom is the Spirit of God? (Genesis 41:38)

Four hundred years later, Moses would lead the children of Israel—now slaves—out of Egypt and across the Red Sea. They spent forty years in the desert. During that time, Moses was becoming exhausted from his responsibilities of judging and administrating the lives of the two million people he'd led out of Egypt. His father-in-law suggested he get others to help him. God agreed to the plan and took of the Holy Spirit that was upon Moses and distributed a portion of the Spirit to seventy helpers!

> Then I will come down and talk with you
> there. I will take of the Spirit that is upon
> you and will put the same upon them; and
> they shall bear the burden of the people with
> you, that you may not bear it yourself alone.
> (Numbers 11:17, 25)

God also put His Holy Spirit on a young man who would become King David. He sent the prophet Samuel to the humble home of a man with several sons including one who would become Israel's next king. One by one, the older sons came before the prophet Samuel but the Spirit of the Lord said, "No, not that one."

Finally, it appeared that all sons had come before Samuel but none were acceptable to the Holy Spirit. When Samuel asked the father if he had any other sons who had not come before him, he said "I have yet one more but he's tending our sheep." The prophet told him to send for him and young David was brought in from herding sheep and anointed to become the next king:

> Then Samuel took the horn of oil and
> anointed him in the midst of his brothers;
> and the Spirit of the Lord came upon David
> from that day forward. So Samuel arose and
> went to Ramah. (1 Samuel 16:13)

King David became the mightiest and godliest king that Israel ever had. He humbled himself before God and was led by His Holy Spirit. On his

31

deathbed, David exalted that the Spirit of the Lord had spoken through his mouth:

> Now these are the last words of David...'The Spirit of the Lord spoke by me, and His word was on my tongue. (2 Samuel 23:1-2)

Elijah, another Old Testament prophet, was also empowered by the Holy Spirit. He was even translated from one place to another by the Spirit:

> And it shall come to pass, as soon as I am gone from you, that the Spirit of the Lord will carry you to a place I do not know; so when I go and tell Ahab, and he cannot find you, he will kill me. But I your servant have feared the Lord from my youth.
> (I Kings 18:12)

In the Book of Nehemiah the people of the Old Testament are told that the Holy Spirit is there to instruct them:

> You also gave Your good Spirit to instruct them, and did not withhold Your manna from their mouth, and gave them water for their thirst. (Nehemiah 9:20)

The Book of Isaiah mentions the Holy Spirit fifteen times, and gives much insight into the nature of the Holy Spirit. That the Holy Spirit was not to depart from the mouth of his descendants' descendants really spoke to me.

> "As for Me,' says the Lord, 'this is My covenant with them: My Spirit who is upon

you, and My words which I have put in your
mouth, shall not depart from your mouth,
nor from the mouth of your descendants, nor
from the mouth of your descendants'
descendants," says the Lord, 'from this time
and forevermore.' (Isaiah 59:21)

Then he remembered the days of old, Moses
and his people, saying: 'Where is He who
brought them up out of the sea with the
shepherd of His flock? Where is He who put
His Holy Spirit within them?' (Isaiah 63:11)

The Book of Ezekiel is called by some '*The Book
of Acts*" of the Old Testament because of the actions
of the Holy Spirit in the prophet Ezekiel's life:

Then the Spirit entered me when He spoke
to me, and set me on my feet; and I heard
Him who spoke to me. (Ezekiel 2:2)

It is in the Book of Joel that the outpouring of the
Holy Spirit the Church is today enjoying can be
seen—with more to come:

And it shall come to pass afterward that I
will pour out My Spirit on all flesh; your
sons and daughters shall prophesy, your old
men shall dream dreams, your young men
shall see visions. And also on My
menservants and on My maidservants I will
pour out My Spirit in those days. (Joel 2:28-
29)

Some of the most famous passages of all about the
Holy Spirit are quoted from the Book of Zechariah:

> So he answered and said to me: This is the
> word of the Lord to Zerubbabel: Not by
> might nor by power, but by My Spirit, says
> the Lord of hosts.' (Zechariah 4:6)

As I finished my Holy Spirit journey through the
Old Testament, I realized more plainly than before
that Jesus had emphasized to His disciples and
followers how important it was that they not try to go
off and start a ministry or a work of their own
without first being empowered by the Holy Spirit.
They were to stay in Jerusalem until *'the promise' of
the Father* had come upon them.[2]

> And being assembled together with them, He
> commanded them ot to depart from Jerusalem,
> but to wait for the Promise of the Father,
> "which," He said, "you have heard from Me;
> for John truly baptized with water, but you
> shall be baptized with the Holy Spirit not
> many days from now."'" (Acts 1:4-5)

Never would I take the Holy Spirit for granted
again. There is nowhere in the Bible where it says the
gifts of the Holy Spirit were to stop. Some
mistakenly quote the following passage in that
manner but a second look at those verses and one
notes that, yes, when that which is perfect has come,
these will all be done away with but what is the
"perfect" that is being referred to?

> But whether there are prophecies, they will
> fail; whether there are tongues, they will
> cease; whether there is knowledge, it will

> vanish away. For we know in part and we
> prophesy in part; but when that which is
> perfect has come, then that which is in part
> will be done away. (I Corinthians 13:8-10)

True, Jesus Christ is perfect but He had already come and provided a perfect atonement for man's sin by that time. So that isn't the 'perfect' to which the above verse refers.

So we have to seek further to find the 'perfect' that will come, causing knowledge, prophecy and tongues to cease.

Obviously, when looked at logically, the 'perfect' referred to in that verse that causes tongues, prophecy and knowledge to cease is at the end of the Age when Jesus Christ comes in the clouds.

Therefore, because the 'perfect' has not yet come, tongues has not yet ceased.

Chapter 4 Endnotes

---

[1] Grudem, Wayne. *Systematic Theology: An Introduction to Biblical Doctrine.* (Grand Rapids, MI. Zondervan. 1995.)
[2] Acts 1:4

5

The Spirit Bade Me Go

One morning a few years ago, I woke up early. I couldn't get back to sleep. I kept thinking about a new book that a friend had given me for Christmas. It was about the Holy Spirit. I could barely put it down.

My thoughts shifted to tomorrow night's Healing Crusade in Cincinnati. I had heard about it on TV and the desire to attend kept crowding in.

But even if I wanted to go, how could I? No. It wouldn't work out. Besides, my husband would never agree on such short notice. After all, I was home-schooling our seven-year old and Chuck would need to go into the office.

I tried to put thoughts of the crusade out of my mind but I was pretty sure the Holy Spirit was nudging me to go—but go a thousand miles away? Besides, I wasn't even sick, why would I go to a healing crusade? I must have misunderstood.

Deep inside though, I knew I hadn't misunderstood. The Holy Spirit was indeed speaking to me. Now as I tried to put down the idea, I was aware of a change inside me, a kind of grieving.

Well, it would never do to grieve someone as lovely as the Holy Spirit. I could *pretend* I hadn't understood the impression I had received; but He knew and I knew that I had very well understood the impression I had received. I decided to test it out.

I decided I would awaken my husband—he was usually awake by now anyway. I did not think he would be in agreement with the idea and I knew that he would put short shrift to the idea if he didn't think I was hearing from the Lord. Besides, if he said no, I would be off the hook.

I had things I would need to prepare if I went. I was a homeschooling mom. I glanced again at the clock: it was only 5:30 AM. Excitement was beginning to rise in me. I went back into the bedroom and gently shook my husband. He opened one eye; rose up on one arm and tried to peer through me to his alarm clock. "It's awfully early, isn't it?" he demanded.

Oh, oh, I thought, this isn't getting me off to a very good start with someone I might have to ask favors of later. I hoped I wasn't just being presumptuous. My no-nonsense engineer husband is a man of few words and he likes things concrete. I was pretty sure I knew what his reaction would be when he found out I had nothing concrete to shore up my strange request.

"Well?" he asked.

"Chuck," I said, "I think the Holy Spirit is telling me to go to the Cincinnati Healing Crusade."

"What is that?" So I told him.

"When is it?"

"Tomorrow," I told him.

"Tomorrow! You've got to be kidding!" He pulled the covers over his head. I had never seen him respond in quite that way before and I thought I must have really shocked him. I hoped he was okay. Wait until he hears I'd need him to stay home and babysit! I knew how busy they were at the office.

When I stopped to think about it, it didn't seem very possible that this would work out. I wondered why the Spirit would ask me to do something like this—if it was the Holy Spirit. What purpose could He possibly have in mind?

True, I had just finished writing a 12-week Bible curriculum on the Holy Spirit for our church's Adult Christian Ed Department. I could have used an experience like this when I was working on the actual writing of it. Then it would have been great to see the Book of Acts displayed before my very eyes. I could easily have made the 12-week course into a 13-week course. All I would have had to do was add a chapter on what the Holy Spirit was doing today.

At Christmastime, knowing I was writing the curriculum, my friend Arlene had given me a just-released book titled *Good Morning, Holy Spirit!* All of our friends were reading it and they were talking about what an awesome book it was. They said it was like He was no longer just a figment of the imagination from ancient biblical texts.

I realized I certainly didn't know Him that well even with all my studying. Yes, indeed, I decided; *I would like to go to that meeting in Cincinnati!*

My friend, Diane, upon learning of my interest in the *Good Morning, Holy Spirit* book had suggested I watch the author's TV show on the Trinity Broadcasting Network. From that time on, as often as I could, I tuned in the show on Saturday nights to watch the move of the Holy Spirit.

There I saw people worshipping Jesus, people getting out of wheelchairs healed and little children laughing and crying as God restored limbs that had never walked. Oh, yes, it seemed to me like it should still be that way today. But—and there were others like me—afraid to follow the inner voice in case we were wrong; afraid we would make a mistake in trying to follow the leading of the Spirit. I guess we didn't take the following Scripture very seriously in those days:

> If a son shall ask bread of any of you that is a father, will he give him a stone? or if he ask a fish, will he for a fish give him a serpent? Or if he shall ask an egg, will he offer him a scorpion? If ye then, being evil, know how to give good gifts unto your children: how much more shall you heavenly Father give the Holy Spirit to them that ask Him? (Luke 11:11-13 kjv)

A week before, I had sensed something was different. It was Saturday and I was watching Benny Hinn's program and preparing dinner at the same time when I felt the touch of the Lord! The presence of the Holy Spirit was overwhelming as it began, inexplicably, to pour out over the airways and into my own little kitchen. As the presence of God increased, I began to weep. Soon I was having trouble standing up. I had to find a chair, or not remain standing. When I was able, I made my way back to our bedroom and lay down.

I pondered the events of that evening now as I stood waiting in our bedroom, making a pretense of picking up a couple of things and straightening the blinds; trying to be quiet while I waited for some response from my usually calm-acting husband.

Suddenly, he sat up. Without even a "Hello, I'm alive and breathing," he said, "Yes. I do think you're supposed to go to Cincinnati." My mouth dropped open.

He told me, "Get ready to leave right away this morning so you can get acclimated before tomorrow night's service."

I stared at him. Could it really be that easy when the Holy Spirit is in something? The thought flashed across my mind that if I hadn't acted on the still small voice of the Spirit, I would have missed out on all this. Inside me, my own spirit was singing, "The Spirit bade me go; the Spirit bade me go."

My husband continued; I was surprised he could move with so much confidence in the Holy Ghost but truly, the Spirit was giving him every necessary detail for my trip. He told me he would stay home and take care of our daughter, adding that he'd been meaning to spend more time with her anyway.

He told me to call the airport and get reservations for this morning. I was to use a travel agency this time to make motel reservations. "Ask for the Holiday Inn nearest the Coliseum," he said.

I didn't have the heart to tell him that I'd heard on TV that every hotel or motel room within a 20-25 mile radius of the Cincinnati Riverfront Coliseum was already booked by crusade-goers. Instead, I just dialed AAA.

When AAA travel agency called me back, they said the Holiday Inn was fully-booked for Thursday night (the night the Crusade began). But then they shared a little known trade secret with me. They said they had taken the liberty to make reservations for Wednesday and Friday evenings in addition to Thursday night. They said I could be pretty sure if I showed up wanting three nights instead of just one, they would accommodate me. Apparently it was the old "a bird in the hand is worth three in the bush" stunt.

By noon that same day, I was at the airport and by 1:00 PM I was winging my way over the continent to Cincinnati. As soon as I arrived, I went to the hotel. I walked into the Holiday Inn and went straight to the desk. I asked the clerk whether they had penciled me in to stay all three nights. The clerk opened the reservations book and then looked at me. I knew he was on to me and that the travel agency's trick wasn't going to work; but all he said was, "You got all three nights, lady."

Suddenly, I was very tired. I went upstairs to my room, unpacked my bag, and promptly fell asleep. I didn't awaken until the next morning. I went downstairs to the motel restaurant for breakfast, ordered a sandwich to go, and left in a cab. I had read that it was a good idea to be in line early if you wanted a good seat. It was only 9:30 AM when I arrived in front of the Coliseum.

6

Good Morning, Holy Spirit

Most of the early birds gathered in front of the coliseum appeared to be veteran crusade-goers. There were two young men who had their sleeping bags beside them. They had obviously spent the night there in their effort to be the first ones in when the doors opened. They came well-supplied with extra Cokes and potato chips. One group brought with them lawn chairs, umbrellas, a jacket, a picnic basket and hot jugs of coffee.

As I looked at those five efficient women, I felt totally inadequate. First, I was dressed too warm in my Minnesota long sleeves. I had neglected to bring sunscreen which my fair skin demanded. I had brought a club sandwich from the restaurant but I had forgotten all about bringing soft drinks until I saw those young men drinking Coke, my favorite.

Oh, they looked good. Now I had eight hours to wait in the sun with nothing to drink. I decided I'd better not eat my sandwich either or I wouldn't be able to stand the thirst.

The ladies around me were peacefully sipping coffee in their own cups and sitting on their own lawn chairs and chatting with friends who had come with them.

The young men soon asked someone to save their spot while they went looking for restrooms. It wasn't long before they came back with the gloomy news that there were no bathrooms to be had. All the doors would be locked until afternoon.

I sat on the concrete sidewalk and took out my book, *Good Morning, Holy Spirit!* I wanted to read it one more time before the Crusade started. The sun was beginning to get hot now. Cincinnati seemed too warm for March. I'm allergic to the sun but my sunscreen was back in my suitcase at the motel. I asked the Lord for help. There was no more space available against the doors or walls of the building where I could be in the shade, and I can have a serious sunburn in 20 minutes or less.

While I wondered what to do, I prayed silently in my prayer language. Soon I spotted one little corner tucked away behind the chairs of the five well-prepared ladies. At the juncture of the first two ladies' chairs, I noticed a decorative wall that jutted out in just such a way as to leave a bit of a recess into which no chair could fit. That, it occurred to me, was the Holy Spirit's provision for me.

I know they thought my request to sit behind them was odd. If we hadn't been at a Christian crusade and all, I might have been turned down; instead they nodded silently and turned back to their friends. I slipped in behind them; and protected by my little wall and their broad backs, I was snug as a bug in a rug—only cooler. It was great.

The day wore slowly on. I never felt too hot again that entire day, even in my long sleeves. Oddly enough, even though I hadn't eaten anything since breakfast, I never felt hunger pangs all that long day. Nor did I feel thirsty. In fact, I was grateful that I hadn't remembered to bring Coke because the two fellows with such an abundant supply were now in misery with no bathrooms in sight! I settled down to read my book and people-observe.

Others began to converse and the distance they had driven or flown to get to the crusade was the object of much "get-acquainted" small talk. Some said they had driven 100 miles or more that very morning because they couldn't find any closer accommodations. I wondered why they hadn't tried the Holiday Inn where I was at, so I asked. "Of course, we tried," they said, "but we were told they hadn't had any rooms available for two or more weeks."

Suddenly, I heard a man shout. People shaded their eyes and looked up where he was excitedly pointing. Other voices, just as excited, joined his. Not wanting to miss anything, I jumped up and squinted into the bright sky. Suddenly, I saw it, too! A perfect rainbow made a circle around the centermost peak of the Cincinnati Riverfront Coliseum. The sky was blue, the sun was streaming down, not a cloud was in the sky; and yet, there hung a beautiful, round, multi-colored rainbow.

The two young men with the sleeping bags could wait no longer. They took off to find bathrooms.

The doors opened around four o'clock, an hour and a half ahead of schedule because of the heat. People pushed their way through the turnstiles and once inside, they began to run down the aisles looking for good seats. I looked around at the huge cavern that seated 18,000 people. Half of it was roped off. The other half was filled with seats and, even as I stood looking around me, people streamed past and took the very places I was contemplating.

Finally, I thought to ask the Holy Spirit where to sit? Immediately, I was directed, in the Spirit, to take a seat near the front but right behind the television camera platform.

At first I thought I hadn't heard Him right. There were only a few bad seats in that whole auditorium and this was one of them. Why would He do this to me after I had been waiting in line for seven hours? I thought for sure He would want me to get a good seat so I could see everything He had brought me a thousand miles, by plane, to see.

I thought I must be hearing wrong, so I asked again. But again, I was impressed with the same instructions. So what could I do? I sat there. I comforted myself with the thought that I had really not come all this way just to see Benny Hinn-the-man anyway. After all, I reasoned, what I needed was to be able to trust the voice of the Holy Spirit! It didn't really matter if I couldn't see those on stage.

I walked over to one of those very bad seats and sat down. I was right; I couldn't see a thing. And everybody seemed to understand that except me. Nonetheless, I stayed. I wanted to be obedient to the leading of the Holy Spirit.

It was now 6 PM and the auditorium was nearly full, even in the area where I was sitting. I had gotten acquainted with some ladies to my right; and now, suddenly, I remembered I was hungry and thirsty. They agreed to hold my seat while I went to get a soft drink.

When I got out into the hall, I saw that enormous tables had been set up and they were full of teaching tapes and books. I walked around the tables; not planning to buy anything. I was just feasting my eyes on the variety of teaching material laid out before me.

As I walked around the tables and looked at what was displayed there, I noticed the Holy Spirit was beginning to instruct me regarding the books and tapes. He would either impress me with, "Get this" or, more likely, "Don't get that." I picked up each thing that He instructed me to, thinking it was just a little exercise in hearing His voice. When I finished my trip around the tables, my hands held several things including a video tape of how to receive the baptism of the Holy Spirit.

As I gazed at them, the Spirit spoke clearly. "Now buy them," He said.

I gulped. I hadn't wanted to spend any more money because I felt we had already done more financially in getting me here than we could afford. I made one excuse after another to the Holy Spirit, suddenly fearing my husband's reaction if I spent more money. Even though fear of spending my husband's money isn't usually one of my virtues— this time it seemed like I just couldn't make myself say yes to the Holy Spirit's leading. An unreasonable concern for money seemed to loom very large before me.

The Holy Spirit put up with my whining for awhile. Then finally, tiring of it, He said in no uncertain terms: "It isn't Chuck's money; *it's My money,* and I say, buy them!" This time, I quickly made the purchases He had shown me and returned to my seat.

Back in my seat, I looked over my purchases. I noticed how accurately the Holy Spirit had assessed what I also considered to be my needs for teaching materials. I was overwhelmed at what a personal God He is. Let me tell you, it was heady.

Technicians were scurrying around now, making final adjustments on the sound system. A couple of musicians were unobtrusively adjusting their instruments. The air was charged with a hushed expectancy. Faith permeated the atmosphere.

By now all the seats around me were taken except that the seat on my left remained empty. I wasn't surprised. Who would want it? I couldn't see anything on stage. (By and by, a man would come by and install a large television screen right beside me and a little over to the right.)

As I was thinking these thoughts, my gaze suddenly shifted to an elderly, somewhat unkempt gentleman who was frantically combing the first ten to fifteen aisles looking for a good seat. He was hoping to find a single seat, unused, up near the front. I thought, that's pretty clever. He's hoping to slip in unobtrusively, even though late, and still get a great seat without waiting! He's braver than I.

He searched for a full five minutes up and down, up and down, before he finally gave up and took the last available seat that was anywhere near close to the speaker's platform. It was the one sitting empty beside me. Never mind that it was behind the cameras where the music team would be obscured from his view, the seat was near the front. He climbed over some people, looking neither to the right nor to the left as he pushed his way in and plunked himself down beside me.

Welcome, I thought silently, we are both Christians...even though you don't seem quite kosher. Then I remembered the ladies who had looked at me with disdain when I'd begged my small little, wonderful corner of shade. I felt contrite. At first I said nothing to him. He must have been 60 years old or older. He was quite disheveled but I didn't think he was a street person, come in off the street for some respite.

I glanced at him out of the corner of my eye; there was a gentle look around his tired eyes. I didn't intend to strike up a conversation, I wanted to just savor the marvelous time I was having with the Holy Spirit. I took out the club sandwich the Holiday Inn had prepared for me some nine hours ago now. I noticed the man seemed hungry.

I looked at my sandwich. I couldn't offer any of it to him, it looked too awful. Anyway, he would probably be offended. When they made the sandwich, they had cut it in two and the bread was not only dry on the top and bottom but also where it was cut. It was filled with this awful grey lettuce and the skinny tomato slice was limp and runny now. The layers and layers of ham still looked okay, though. I knew ham didn't spoil easily. I stripped off the garnish and took a bite. Suddenly I felt really hungry. The potato chips still looked good, too.

I noticed that the man sitting beside me kept inadvertently eyeing my sandwich. Every time I took a bite, his eyes would travel to my mouth and then hastily look away and then back again. I pretended not to notice while I figured out what to do. Obviously, he had no time for dinner. I finished the first half of the sandwich and then, getting up my courage, I turned to him and in a very nonchalant manner, I said, "I am so full. I hate to see this other half go to waste, but I don't suppose you would want to eat it, would you?—*it is* kind of stale."

He protested politely at first then quickly accepted it before I changed my mind. It delighted me to see him eating it. He said he hadn't had a chance to eat anything since noon, and he rapidly downed it. Having eaten my sandwich, he felt compelled to carry on a polite conversation with me. I soon learned that his parents had come over from the Old Country and that he was a new Christian.

He said he was from the Cincinnati area and still attended the same Greek Orthodox Church where his parents had taken him as a babe. He had been an altar boy there, too, he said. Then he had married a wonderful Greek girl but had shamed the family when his wife divorced him because of some "bad things" he had done, (and here the old gentlemen hung his head, overcome by grief and shame).

When he had composed himself again, he said that even though he'd gone to church since he was a boy, he had never understood spiritual things. That is, until a couple of years ago when his Greek Orthodox Church had gotten a new priest who had started giving services in English as well as Greek. Then the old man had found Christ as Lord and Saviour. He looked up at me with his tired old eyes, but he was beaming now. He began to glow as he talked about His Jesus.

This new priest was trying to teach his people about the baptism of the Holy Spirit. "But," said the old man, "it is hard for us to understand that it is for today."

The Holy Spirit spoke distinctly to me, "Give him that video tape series on the baptism of the Holy Spirit that you just purchased." "No" was the first thing that went through my mind; I wanted it for my relatives out in the Wisconsin Bible study. Did the Holy Spirit want me to give it up?

"Give it to him," the Holy Spirit repeated. And, of course, I did. I reached into my bag and turned to the little, old man and said, "I think the Spirit is telling me to give this to you for your priest...so he can teach you and so you can have the Holy Spirit, too." The man looked at me in surprise as though he wasn't used to taking gifts from strangers and then decided it was okay. In the next moment, he was thanking me profusely.

I felt good about it. I knew that the priest had a big enough job bringing people to salvation where it had not been taught before; thank God for a man that was trying to bring this dear little Greek man and others like him, into the fullness of the Spirit!

The meeting was about to begin. There was a breathless expectancy in the people. And so much hope. I guess you could say the air was pregnant with faith. I leaned back and closed my eyes, hoping I was sending a signal to the little man of my unwillingness to communicate further. He seemed to understand and clutched his video. I just wanted to experience the presence of the Lord.

Suddenly, without warning, the Holy Spirit began to heal some little things in me. It had nothing to do with Benny Hinn. Benny Hinn would not even come out onto the platform for another thirty minutes. I looked around. It was awesome. Healings were beginning to happen spontaneously all over the Coliseum. The music began, the singing started and a half hour later, Benny came on stage. You could tell that Benny knew the Lord. He told us he could do nothing, only the Lord could heal us. As we worshiped, healings continued to happen all around the auditorium At least twelve people got up out of wheelchairs that night.

After a long while, it was offering time. I asked the Lord, "How much shall I give?" And He said to me, "$60 cash." Just as clear as could be, the Spirit told me $60 cash. I hadn't planned to give that much and my thoughts rushed back to what my husband would think but I struggled only briefly this time. "Okay, Lord." I knew I had more than that with me.

As Benny Hinn talked about the offering, he explained that none of the money being collected would go to him because he is supported by the church he pastors. All the money collected would go to missions and to finance the Crusade.

But his next statement floored me. Just when I was beginning to feel so comfortable, that I could really hear the small still voice of the Lord, Benny Hinn said, "The Holy Spirit has told me to ask everyone that can, to give $100 or more this evening."

I was devastated. I knew the Holy Spirit had told *me* to give $60 cash. That meant that either Benny Hinn or I were not hearing from the Spirit. I couldn't even contemplate that, I was so crushed. My heart plummeted to the depths in one small moment. I had come with hope and that was to learn whether or not I, an ordinary person, could hear from the Holy Spirit. Now it seemed that Benny Hinn had heard something that didn't confirm what I thought I'd heard. How could I have been fooled? It was such a disappointment; I don't know when I've felt so sad.

But then I heard the Holy Spirit's small, soft voice again. "Child," He said, "how much did Benny Hinn ask you to give?"

"One hundred dollars or more."

"And how much did I just tell you to give?"

"$60 Cash—I thought that was what I heard."

"And how much did that video on the baptism cost that you gave to that old gentleman?"

"$44.00," I said.

"Now, add them up," He said in His quiet voice.

Suddenly, I gasped. Why, if you added the $60 in cash that the Spirit had told me to put into the offering plate plus the $44 cost for the video tapes, it did add up to more than $100.00. *Both* Benny Hinn and I had heard right! Benny had integrity and I could hear the voice of the Lord!!

My faith came rushing back in—the Holy Spirit had used this unusual way to confirm that I was really hearing His voice!

What an awesome God—the same yesterday, today and tomorrow. He still wants to empower His people and use them in the same way as He did in the Old Testament.

Yes, sir, Old Testament Gideon and I *could both hear* from the Holy Spirit....!

7

The Conference Continues

The next morning, I again arrived early. Going into the half-filled auditorium, I started to go back to the seat I had sat in the night before where I had been so especially blessed. But then I thought, "No, I should ask Him again."

This time the Holy Spirit directed me toward the back, kind of in the center, but again a place where nobody else was sitting. By now, I had learned that if I obeyed, I was in for a treat.

By and by, some African-American women came in and after some conversation decided to sit down in my same section. One was sitting right beside me and her friend was to the left of her. I don't know if the woman beside me was physically beautiful or if it was because she was so holy and godly that she seemed beautiful. But the three of us were soon in deep conversation while we waited for the Friday morning teaching session to begin.

Little by little they shared about their families and I began to share about mine. We had a beautiful twenty-three year old daughter who was home again, unmarried and pregnant. The young man was unsuitable at that time for a husband. How our daughter grieved that she could have fallen for him when she had such a strong missionary call on her life, one that she had nurtured and prepared for all her life. There seemed no way out but for her to marry the young man, ignore his love of drinking and carousing, and spend the rest of her life supporting him and any other children they might have.

But as I shared our sorrow at the life that seemed to lay ahead for our older daughter, these two black women just seemed to emanate empathy. Later as I thought about it, I understood the heart cry of the black woman. They have been through this generation after generation. They have raised beautiful children with so much tender love and compassion and energy, only to leave them unguided as they are forced outside their home to feed their families; leaving children open to drugs and out-of-wedlock pregnancies.

They also had generations of wisdom to pass on to me. They said, "You give this message to your daughter. Tell her that if the young man is not everything she would want in a husband if she wasn't in this situation, she isn't to accept him. He doesn't have a right to her just because he made her pregnant. Tell her to wait for the right man to come along or live singly. Either way, she'll be better off."

Somehow I believed them, and I took the message home to my despairing daughter. My daughter gave birth to a beautiful little girl and raised her in the

Lord and this fall, our granddaughter left for Bible college with plans to be a missionary.

Benny Hinn was beginning to teach the group assembled there on how to receive "the anointing" from the Holy Spirit. He taught for awhile from Scripture, saying "the anointing" only comes to those who are willing to give up all for the Holy Spirit. As he finished, he blew upon the audience, saying, "Receive your anointing by the power of the Holy Spirit." I looked around me in amazement; whole sections of people began to look startled and then fall over backwards onto their chairs. He blew again towards first one section then another and as before; each section, row by row, would topple over! "Receive your anointing," he said over and over again.

At first, I was a little skeptical and wondered if I would fall if he blew my way. But as my section began toppling, the first row and then the second and on and on, all by the one breath of air, I suddenly felt a cool wind reach me and then I was down, too. As I was going down, I remember thinking, "Hmmm, this is interesting."

When the Friday morning session finished, I caught a cab outside the Coliseum. On the way back to my hotel, my cab driver asked me to show him how to get eternal life. I led him to Jesus and prayed with him. With the anointing, it was easy as pie.

8

Living in the Anointing

That night, I went back to the Coliseum for the final meeting. Again, I asked the Holy Spirit where I should sit. I was impressed that I should sit high up towards the back of the auditorium.

By now, my expectations were high. The service was again wonderful and many were being healed and having personal experiences with the Lord but nothing special was happening to me. I found myself left with a vague feeling of uneasiness.

I wondered how I could be feeling that way when there was such beautiful singing and worshiping going on and people were being healed right before my eyes. The disappointment stemmed from the fact that there was no *personal interaction* going on between the Holy Spirit and me. I had quickly gotten used to living in the anointing and *I hated it* when I had to do without that close walk between my Lord and me.

Besides, I had been feeling special. I realized that I had expected Him to do something *really spectacular* this last night of the Benny Hinn Healing Crusade, you know, to kind of finish it up royally.

For most of the service, there wasn't even anybody sitting in the seat beside me. I have to say, I was a little bit petulant.

About halfway through the service, a woman came rushing in. She plopped down beside me and began to undo her jacket, then carefully laid it beside her. She looked around trying to get acclimated, I suppose, and half-heartedly joined in the singing. She drummed her fingertips, just a little bit, on the arm of the seat furthest from me. I could tell she was a nervous sort and yet she was there for a purpose. I knew within myself she had a real need.

I could tell my new neighbor was having trouble settling down and letting go the cares of the day to concentrate on the Lord. Finally, it was getting toward the end of the healing testimonials when Benny Hinn asked everybody to stand up and again receive the anointing. "Even those way back in the back of the bleachers," he said. That was us.

At first I didn't think the lady beside me was going to stand. I guess she felt silly but finally she stood, maybe so that she didn't look conspicuous. Benny Hinn again blew though the microphone, first toward one side of the auditorium and then the other. Most of the people began to fall again in that domino effect for which he is known, as the Holy Spirit came upon them. You could tell that the Spirit was real because the people seemed to fall row by row as the Spirit moved backward in the auditorium.

It seemed like it took a long time for the Spirit to get back to us but suddenly I found myself going over with a bang against the back of my chair. I wasn't expecting this. Because we were so far back, I'd felt my personal move of the Spirit was over. Now I began to weep as the anointing came upon me.

After a bit, I became aware that the lady beside me had not received anything. Everyone else had gone over when the wind of the Spirit hit their row but she stalwartly remained standing. The Lord told me to tell her that He loved her, too, since she hadn't been able to receive from Him directly herself. I was ready to lean over and whisper words that I believed were coming up out of my Spirit that were intended for her. Suddenly I noticed she had flounced off.

She was gone but He had set her beside me especially so I could personally pass on words from Him to her so that she would hear what He wanted to say to her. It wasn't too unusual for me to sometimes get a simple message from the Lord for someone else but this time, I never had a chance to give her the message. He had wanted to tell her that He loved her and that He is not a respecter of persons and that she was as acceptable to Him as anyone else at the conference. But it was too late. She was gone. Would she turn away from Him now? I hoped not.

Everybody was leaving. The Crusade was over. It was dark outside now. There were a few people here and there, talking in clusters, as they tried to hail a cab. A cab pulled up beside me and the driver asked if I minded sharing a cab with two other people. Of course, I didn't; cabs were in short supply.

The cabdriver left me off last and while he was driving to the motel, he plied me with questions about the Crusade and Benny Hinn and about salvation. He said he wished all his clients were like the ones he had picked up after the meetings. He said they were different and he asked me what made them different. I told him and I asked him if he wanted Jesus to come into his heart.

"No," he said, "I ain't never heard about this Jesus this way before and I want to make sure it's the right way before I do it cause I've got a wife and two kids at home that's dependin' on me."

"I've got a Bible you can have," I said, handing over my new gilt-edged New Testament.

"Oh," he said, "that's too purty." I assured him it wasn't and he said, "Well, I'm gonna take good care of it and not get any spots on it from my fingers."

This uneducated man longed for truth. I could tell. His heart was *so beautiful...and he had never heard the gospel before that night.*

He dropped me off and very, very soberly, I walked into the motel. I hoped the anointing would never leave me.

64

9
A Little Girl's Surprise for Mom & Dad

The Holy Spirit was wonderful in Cincinnati! I saw such wonderful things happen to people! So many were set free from cancer or from crippling diseases or from emotional restraints. They were sheep without a shepherd until they called upon their heavenly Father and He took them and shouldered their responsibilities and tended them.

Many people got up out of wheelchairs and walked that night. But I remember in particular one bouncy little 4-year old girl. At least, she had springs in her knees that night after she received her healing. Actually, she had never walked before in her whole life. Her parents weren't believers so the little girl's babysitter had brought her to the healing crusade. Her mom and dad had wanted to go out for a date night so they told the teenage girl that if she would babysit for them that night, she could just take the little girl along with her to the healing crusade.

The teenager, who happened to be a Christian, said "Sure" and asked three of her girlfriends who were also Christians to go with her. They had all jumped in a car and driven into Cincinnati that night, taking with them the crippled child of unsaved parents. What a celebration that must have been when the parents returned from their party to find four teen-age girls and discovered their "miracle baby!" The mom and dad must have danced and cried with joy to hear the good news that God had sovereignly healed their little girl as she sat in the audience with legs that had never once walked in four years. Now she had been miraculously healed!

She and the four teenagers stood in a long line of people that night waiting to testify to what the Lord had done for their small charge. I had watched as the ecstatic little four-year old ran back and forth, back and forth, jumping up and down, trying out her new knees and legs. When the five of them finally got to the front where Benny Hinn was interviewing those claiming healings, the little girl whirled and twirled on brand new legs while the babysitter and her friends proudly showed Benny their miracle!

I know that in New Testament times, there must have been just that same kind of joy and flow of excitement as Jesus healed and drove out demons and told of the Kingdom of Heaven that all could enter if they would only believe—it must have been just the way I saw it happen that night in Cincinnati!

PART II

STUDYING

10
Gifts from God

I was discovering that with the baptism of the Holy Spirit comes a deep and abiding desire to read the Bible. He also gives peace inside. The more one prays 'in the Spirit,' the more one is able to rise above the problems of life and are able to defeat the troublesome areas in our life and that of our family.

The Holy Spirit of God is an unobtrusive friend. He is a continual refreshing in an ever-living atmosphere of hope that envelops us wherever we go. I have never been without the fullness of the Holy Spirit since I've been born again so I don't know what it's like to believe in Jesus but not have a prayer language.

I no longer know what it's like to be without the myriad of ideas that comes forward to solve the problems that come up in my life as in everyone's life. I learned in the years after I discovered the treasure of talking in tongues myself that a local Minneapolis-area pastor needed to enlarge his church for his growing congregation. All he had to work with was a hopeless-looking warehouse. Today it is above-gorgeous; it even houses a bubbling water fountain in an atrium—all ideas he attributes to the Holy Spirit while praying in tongues.

Now that I had some Bible teaching, I was more aware that the desire of the Spirit of the Lord is that He be my Helper, my Advocate, my Comforter and my Standby. That was what Jesus was trying to explain to His disciples when He told them about the coming Holy Spirit before His crucifixion. He told them His whole walk and ministry had been empowered by the Holy Spirit.

He had been trying to model for them how one walks with the Holy Spirit in real life. He gave the Holy Spirit high ratings in His conversation with His disciples as He was preparing to return to the Father. He said He would be sending the Spirit who would personally indwell each of them just as in the Old Testament the Spirit had indwelt the priests, prophets and kings of ancient Israel—and had empowered His ministry, too, allowing Him to heal the sick and raise the dead back to life.

The disciples must have understood, at least partially, what that was going to mean to them. They had seen Jesus operate in a supernatural way all during the three years of His ministry here on earth even though they probably hadn't fully understood at first. But over the next three years they had become acquainted with the work of the Spirit as they watched Him raise dead men to life, seen Him heal the blind and the lepers and call life into the limbs of the crippled.

Now Jesus was telling them that this same Comforter would be present in their lives to assist them in their walk as Christians. Excitement must have been running very high. From His statement to

70

His disciples, it was clear that Jesus felt this new arrangement would be better for them than when He, as just one person, had been trying to interact with all of them. Now they could each have a one-on-one relationship with the Lord.

> [Jesus said] "Nevertheless, I tell you the truth; It is expedient for you that I go away: for if I go not away, the Comforter will not come unto you; but if I depart, I will send him unto you." (John 16:7 KJV)

In another version of the Bible, the *Amplified Bible,* an even more in-depth explanation of the personality of the Holy Spirit (the Greek word is "*paraclete*" is given. The word is translated "Comforter" in the King James Bible) and it helps us understand what the Christian had to look forward to after Jesus returned to Heaven and sent the Holy Spirit in His place:

> [Jesus said] However, I am telling you nothing but the truth when I say it is profitable (good, expedient, advantageous) for you that I go away. Because if I do not go away, the Comforter (Counselor, Helper, Advocate, Intercessor, Strengthener, Standby) will not come to you [into close fellowship with you]; but if I go away, I will send Him to you [to be in close fellowship with you]."
> (John 16:7 AMP)

In analyzing Jesus' words to His disciples, it is hard to misunderstand the importance of the Holy Spirit. Jesus taught His followers to wholeheartedly embrace the teaching, assisting and comforting presence of the indwelling Holy Spirit. Simply put, a treasure was being sent back to earth after His ascension whose presence would greatly enhance our lives. The attributes of this presence can be understood by looking at the word *Paraklete,* translated 'Comforter' and described in *The Amplified Version* of the Bible.

- <u>Comforter</u>: One who gives contentment and consolation.
- <u>Counselor</u>: Giver of advice and recommendation when consulted.
- <u>Helper</u>: One who accomplishes work to attain an end.
- <u>Advocate</u>: Public defender and vindicator in another's cause.
- <u>Intercessor</u>: One who makes petitions on another's behalf.
- <u>Strengthener</u>: One who resists attacks and intervenes for another.
- <u>Standby</u>: One who can be relied upon in an emergency.

Now I was beginning to study the Bible for hours each day. I attended prayer meetings whenever I could and was at our own church for every possible sermon. I could not get enough of the wonderful things I was learning.

I could see that the Old Testament Jew knew all about the coming of the Holy Spirit centuries before it happened. Although their spirits had not been renewed because they had not accepted the born again experience nor had they accepted Jesus as Messiah, yet they understood certain things given through their Old Testament prophets that made them await the Holy Spirit's coming with anticipation and patience.

Yet when their Messiah did come, they couldn't or wouldn't receive Him because He had come as humble Savior and Lord and not as a conquering king. They have continued to search for someone else whom they believe better fits the description of who they believed their Messiah would be.[1] Even today, two thousand years later, they are still awaiting His first coming as we await the same Messiah at His Second Coming.

They knew intellectually that it was God's Spirit that hovered over the surface of the waters as the creation was being formed. The *King James Version* calls it "brooding," a term familiar to those of us raised on a farm where, as an example, a mother hen broods over her chicks—covering them with her wings for protection.[2]

He also garnished—beautified—the heavens for our enjoyment.[3] He appeared as a cloud by day and a pillar of light by night, enabling Moses to lead the children of Israel out of Egypt and into the Promised Land.[4] He enabled artisans to make beautiful fabric to be used in the Tabernacle, and enabled them to create things of beauty through inner knowledge extended to them supernaturally by the Holy Spirit.[5]

First Saul and then David the Shepherd boy were anointed by the Holy Spirit to serve as kings of Israel.[6] The prophet Ezekiel revealed in words given him by the Holy Spirit that one day God would put His Presence in ordinary laypeople.[7] The Prophet Joel was given the same information.[8]

When Jesus came asking John the Baptist to baptize Him, He was first baptized in water. Afterward He was also baptized with the Holy Spirit.[9] From then on, in every aspect of His life and ministry, the Lord Jesus Christ constantly depended upon the Holy Spirit. His first miracle, turning water into wine, was not done until *after* He received the baptism of the Holy Spirit.[10]

Therefore, how much more does today's believer need to rely upon and continually look to the Holy Spirit for strength, wisdom, power, guidance, and victory?

- Jesus was born of the Spirit (Mt. 1:18-20)
- Jesus was filled with the fullness of the Spirit (Jn. 3:34)
- Jesus was led by the Holy Spirit (Lk. 4:1)
- Jesus was empowered by the Spirit (Lk. 4:14)
- Jesus was anointed by the Holy Spirit (Lk. 4:18; Acts 10:38)
- Jesus was baptized with the Holy Spirit (Acts 1:5)

- Jesus preached and taught by the Spirit (Lk.4:18)
- Jesus healed the sick by the Spirit (Acts 10:38)
- Jesus cast out demons by the Spirit (Mt. 12:28)
- Jesus was offered on the Cross by the Spirit (Heb.9:14)
- Jesus was resurrected by the Spirit (Rom.8:11)
- Jesus used the Holy Spirit to give orders to His disciples (Acts 1:2)
- Jesus baptized His followers with the Holy Spirit (Acts 1:5, 8)
- Even today Jesus governs and directs the affairs of the Church by the Holy Spirit (Jn. 1416; Rev.2:7, 11)

On the day when Jesus ascended back into heaven, He told His followers that in a few days He would send the Holy Spirit to them.[11]

He told them not to leave Jerusalem until this happened.[12]

Chapter 10 Endnotes

---

[1] First 5 books of the Old Testament which were given directly to Moses by God.
[2] Luke 13:34
[3] Job 26:13
[4] Exodus 13:21, 22
[5] Exodus 31:1, 2
[6] I Samuel 10:1-6; I Samuel 16:13
[7] Ezekiel 36:26, 27
[8] Joel 2:28, 29
[9] Luke 3:16; 21, 22
[10] John 1:32, 32; 2:1
[11] Luke 24:49; John 14:26
[12] Acts 1:4, 8

11

Miracles Start Happening

My personal life was changing, too, after I began using tongues on a regular basis. Praying in tongues not only calms us, they break down barriers in the unseen world around us. The Bible also says that praying in tongues 'edifies' us inside.

> He who speaks in a tongue edifies himself, but he who prophesies edifies the church...he who prophesies is greater than he who speaks in tongues, unless indeed he interprets, that the church may receive edification.
> (I Corinthians 14:4-5)

The above passage speaks of two kinds of edification. One is received when a word of prophecy is spoken in a church service, the other—the gift of tongues—edifies the person speaking at any time that he chooses to pray using his prayer language.

At first I wondered what the word 'edifies' meant because I knew I didn't know what I was saying when I was speaking/praying in tongues yet Scripture said I was 'edified' when I spoke in tongues. I looked up the word 'edified' and this is what I found:

> EDIFICATION (GR. *Oikodomeo*) "To build a
> house, tower, town, and so forth (Mt.7:24, 26):
> to build in a spiritual sense, as the Church
> (Mt.16:18), to profit spiritually, to edify…a
> house, a dwelling."[1]

By that time, many years had passed and I was a carpooling mom for our youngest. Every day during the school year I was on call; first, to drive our daughter to school and then to pick her up at the end of the day—at least a twenty mile round trip, twice a day; day-after-day.

The routine cut into everything that I would otherwise have been doing but it seemed to be the most important thing I could be doing at that stage in our daughter's life as it was a Christian school. Our two older children had long since left the nest and we were trying to do things a little differently, a little better (or so we thought) for this our youngest by nearly twenty years.

Because I spent so much time on the road during the school year that I might otherwise have spent in Bible study (my passion) and prayer, I coveted the news that a neighboring church had opened their sanctuary so anyone who wanted could slip in and pray between the hours of 6 and 8 am every morning, Monday through Friday..

I was one of the few who took advantage of that space and all that summer, I was over there praying in tongues for two whole hours, week after week. I enjoyed it so much. One day, as I faithfully kept this commitment, I had an interesting thing happen to me.

I guess people that know call it an *open vision*. It wasn't just a dream; it was like I was actually a part of what was happening.

As I was walking back and forth and quietly praying in tongues, I noticed an angel—a group of angels. They were clad in white and had wings and there were multitudes congregated above me as if we were at an airport and planes were flying overhead. They were flying in a pattern similar to how planes at the airport might fly as they circled, waiting for their turn to come in for a landing.

The angels circled in a pattern until their turn to land came. Then, as fast as they could, they would come in for a landing beside me; digging their heels into the ground to slow them down as they skidded to a halt. Then they would cup their hand to their ear to better hear what I was praying and zoom off again and another would take their place. (I was praying in the Spirit, in my heavenly language.)

This did not seem at all strange to me. I knew that Jesus 'ever liveth to make intercession' for the saints. This was the Spirit of Jesus who was praying through me, I was just supplying the vocalization. It seemed that the words I was praying were giving instructions to angels on assignment.

I have always believed that man cannot tell angels what to do—only God can. This seemed to bear that out. When we pray in tongues we are allowing the Holy Spirit to pray out through us. It was He from whom they were taking instruction from the prayers I was praying in my unknown language, but inspired by Him.

As soon as they heard a piece of what I was saying, they would take off again, as swift as they could to carry out the instructions they apparently were receiving from God through my prayers. As one left, another angel would come zooming in; get an assignment and, with great urgency, take off again. Another from those circling above would come in and the process would be repeated over and over again.

It was from this that I learned that one of the 'varieties' of tongues—the Bible says these unknown tongues are of men and of angels[2]—can be used by the Spirit of God to give angels their operating instructions so that they can go about their business. I speak the words with my vocal cords but it is the Holy Spirit who is speaking through me.

This is one more way that the Bible says angels are 'ministering spirits' to the heirs of salvation.[3] It must be that we speak out His plan in tongues, through God's Holy Spirit—allowing Him to give His angels instructions through our prayers. What if we don't pray in tongues but quote Bible verses with promises in them? That's good, too, but more laborious.

This made me even more interested in the fact that in the Book of Philippians we are told to pray continually. Prior to my experience with the angels, I had wondered how anyone could possibly 'pray continually' but now I understand that this is easy for

80

a Christian to do. Because tongues are from the Spirit of God within, it bypasses my human intellect. Somehow, don't ask me how; I am able to write out a grocery list while silently praying in tongues. I guess it's just one more miracle of God!

Now, I would be the first to admit that speaking in different languages that I never studied is not the only gift of the Spirit, but because most books on the Holy Spirit emphasize the other eight gifts of the Spirit and almost bypass the gift of an unknown language, I don't want to do that. Speaking in tongues is given to us when we believe and it is the gift we can activate and use any time we want, unlike some of the others.

Many people keep a generator on their premises. If the electricity goes out during a storm or a hurricane, they can go and start their generator. That generator gives out energy to run their lights, their refrigerator, their freezer, hair dryer and a myriad of other things so that they are completely empowered in their homes even though their neighbors may be without power.

In a sense, that is what the Holy Spirit is to the Christian. Tongues not only edify and build us up; they also are our *power source* as we pray. In fact, the more we pray, the more we are able to discern things, decide things and come up with new ways to run our lives. We seem to have a perfect and close connection to the God-inside-us when we pray in tongues—and if we're listening for His help—the Holy Spirit will show us the way of escape just when we need it!!!

One time, my 15-year old daughter and I were headed south 300-miles to attend my nephew's wedding in Madison, Wisconsin. My husband and adult son had left the previous day because my son was going to sing for his wedding. The bride was from a Southeast Asian country and she was having a Buddhist wedding for her parents' sake before my nephew and his bride celebrated a second wedding ceremony in the Lutheran church they attended, with his father, as Lutheran pastor, officiating.

We headed out early that Saturday morning with the intent of arriving just before the wedding started that evening at 7:00. All the way down, I felt such an urgency to pray in the Spirit. I enlisted my daughter to help me pray about "something" that seemed very urgent, but I did not know what.

Hours into the drive, I found out. Our car began to smoke. There was nowhere to pull over. We were in an isolated area and had been in a road repair zone for hours. One half of the four-lane freeway was blocked off and the two lanes that were open had disgruntled drivers going both ways sixty miles an hour, bumper-to-bumper.

My car began to make grinding noises. To add to my distress there was a lake or a dark swamp running right alongside the road on the right-hand side of the road with no place to turn off.

The traffic behind us was impatient with the frequent delays and they sped in the opposite direction going north while I had to drive at a minimum of 65 miles per hour going south or I would have caused a huge pile-up of cars traveling bumper-to-bumper behind me.

By now my car was beginning to smoke and make coughing sounds. There was nowhere to turn off. Cars in front of me and behind me and beside me going in the opposite direction. I was praying fast and furious. I didn't know what to do.

Finally, just as my car sputtered and died; one small clearing in all that roadwork and water showed up on the side of the road. I rolled to the edge, perhaps only as much as six inches off the roadway. We were in grave danger. If any car, in either direction had made the tiniest error in driving judgment in the next several hours as they sped past us—it would have all been over.

After two or three hours, I tried starting my car again. It had cooled just enough so I was able to move it over about two feet off the roadway and then it died, not to rise again.

I am convinced that it was because of just such a problem lying ahead of us that I did not know about but which the Holy Spirit did, that I had felt the frantic need to pray those hours in tongues. But God is good and He got me to the little area where I could get off and wait for assistance.

Someone finally thought to call the highway patrol for us—I did not yet have a cell phone at the time—and he arrived and called a tow truck for us. Lucky for us, we arrived at the wedding just in time to shower, put on a pretty dress and show up at the wedding afterglow—and our AAA travel plan paid for all the towing.

It was a wonderful example of the Holy Spirit knowing what lie ahead for us and arranging all the details so that we were safe. I wouldn't trade *anything* for the indwelling Holy Spirit who is able to intercede for us through unknown languages when we have not even a clue as to why we feel the urgency to pray!

Another time when the Holy Spirit was so evidently watching out for me was when I was going for a walk and several houses down our street there was a house where there was often trouble and the police called. As I passed the yard, I heard snarling and looked over just in time to see a large dog coming from behind the house. I started praying rapidly in tongues because the dog seemed so vicious.

The Holy Spirit had prepared me ahead of time. I had read a book in which the author wrote that one could pray in tongues and bind the power of Satan so the demons inside a person (or dog?) would have to cease their activity at the name of Jesus.

I was glad I'd read that because I had only moments to put it to the test. The dog charged across the lawn toward me. I'd started silently praying in tongues as soon as I saw the danger, now as the dog came toward me, I said, 'In the name of Jesus, I bind you, Satan.' The demon spirit in the dog immediately shut down.

The dog stopped in its tracks and whined; it was like it didn't know what to do next, like it couldn't figure out how it got there or what was happening. And, indeed, it was like a giant piece of plexiglass had been dropped down between the dog and I.

The owner's door flew open and an angry and scruffy man came rushing out, grabbed the dog by the collar and dragged him back into the house and slammed the door.

Believe me, no apology expected. I went off down the street and finished my walk.

Chapter 11 Endnotes

---

[1] *Hebrew-Greek Key Word Study Bible, kjv,* 1741.
[2] I Corinthians 13:1
[3] Hebrews 1:14

12

More Miracles

There was another time when I had to rely on God's Holy Spirit by praying in tongues to keep from being attacked by a dog. Actually, it was two dogs that time.

I was staying at Christian Retreat in northern Minnesota to get some writing done in the peace and quiet of the woodsy setting. I decided to go for a walk. It was a peaceful day, sunshiny and beautiful with green grass and trees and swamps on both sides of the dirt road.

The water was black and the lily pads had shiny green leaves with a long stem reaching into the recesses of the murky pond. Occasionally a frog would jump off a pad and there would be the sound of an ever-widening series of ripples. I could hear something like crickets or birds chirping as I walked along.

Suddenly the tranquility was broken. I heard loud barking, then I heard snarling as two dogs came rushing toward me from an old farmhouse up the road. I could see their teeth. They had broken their chains and they were coming for me. I knew I was in trouble but I didn't know what to do.

I looked behind me. Another walker was a block or two behind me. She hesitated. I knew she wanted to help but was torn between helping me and running toward camp in the opposite direction to get help. I waved her back. She was too far back to be of any help and anyway there were two dogs—there was one to attack each of us if she tried to come to my rescue.

I remember being very calm as I prayed in tongues. I didn't know what to do. I remembered the other time I had been attacked by a vicious dog. I had shouted, "Satan, I bind you in Jesus' name!" It might have sounded silly if there had been anyone around to hear me, but again, this had an effect on these two dogs. They paused for just a split second but kept coming.

Now an additional thought came to me—"Lunge toward them." So I did it. They hesitated just a moment longer before starting toward me again. I did it again while shouting, "Go home!" Using the name of Jesus again and again—and lunging a foot or two toward them each time. The snarling stopped and they finally turned tail and ran.

By the time I got back to the Retreat Center, I was famous. The other walker had rushed back and notified the staff of my plight. The sheriff had been called and he said one of the dogs had attacked another walker the summer before and his owner was under strict orders to keep him chained at all times. Actually, the owner had chained *both* dogs but they'd broken their chains. Once more I thanked God for His unexpected protection so far from home.

Another even more unlikely miracle happened in that same area. Our prayer language is such a great aid to immediately connect us to God when we need help. Because it is the Holy Spirit within, first of all assessing my need and, second, giving me the words to pray to the Father; my mind is by-passed and my prayers are completely accurate—a miracle in itself.

Besides, the Holy Spirit knows how to pray better than I do; His prayers are a million times more creative than mine. In the incident I am about to relate, it would never have occurred to me to ask God for a brand new, spanking white and chrome monster-size pickup truck to come up behind me in a narrow gravel road and rescue me from a would-be assailant. Anyway I'm not that bold in my prayer life to think up an idea that far out of the box but evidently the Holy Spirit could and would.

Despite these incidents, the retreat center is one of my favorite spots for writing. It is so peaceful, meals are supplied, there is a lake nearby and it has great Christian speakers every morning and evening during the summer. It is located inside an Indian reservation about twenty-five miles from a tourist town. One has to turn off at a one-gas pump grocery store to catch the road that leads into the backwoods camp.

I tend to be directionally-challenged which is why my husband has a GPS system installed in all our vehicles. That summer, the road that went through the center of town was under construction. This was confusing to me as I was forced to take an unknown road in my attempt to safely navigate my way back to where I would be staying.

Somehow I got off on a wrong road and was zigzagging back and forth on winding dirt roads trying to find the little unmarked road that leads to camp. As the camp is quite remote, the road is gravel with two narrow lanes. There are swamps and ponds on both sides as it winds through some great scenery boxed in with beautiful, dark woods.

I was so lost, even my GPS wasn't tracking. It was late afternoon and I worried that I wouldn't get to camp before dark because I felt it was unsafe to be out there after dark. I knew I was in trouble and was praying in tongues during the whole time.

Suddenly, something happened that deeply alarmed me. I saw an old rusty pickup truck up ahead and it seemed to be slowing down. The man looked evil and I could tell he was watching me in his side view mirror. Slower and slower he drove.

By now I was madly praying in tongues. I didn't know what to do. There was no place to turn around. The road was too narrow and I couldn't pass him because he was driving in the middle of the road. Finally, I had to drop my speed down to about 20 miles an hour because that's how slow he was going. There were tall trees on both sides of the road with an occasional two-tire path leading off into the woods. I continued to pray in tongues, wondering that this was all happening. It was like a movie playing out.

Suddenly I could see in the pickup's side mirror that the man was no longer watching me. His eyes did a double-take. He was looking at something behind me. This caused me to look in my own rearview mirror. There I saw the greatest sight I could possibly have seen at that moment—a great big, shiny-white, monster-sized pick-up truck was following right on my bumper. I remember noticing that my car and the pick-up in front of me were dirty from the dusty roads but this white-and-chrome vehicle was shiny clean. It didn't have a spot of dust on it.

At first I was just relieved. I thought, "Oh, good, the guy ahead of me will have to move over to let the white pickup truck pass and I'll stick right behind the white pickup and pass him at the same time."

I could still see the guy's face in the side mirror of the old pickup truck in front of me. He looked terrified. He sped up and a short ways ahead, he pulled over into an almost invisible two-tire path leading into the forest and disappeared from sight.

I looked behind me but the white shiny truck was nowhere to be seen. Believe me; I thanked God for my prayer language and for His deliverance that day!

And when I did, I was surprised that He responded to me by saying (impressing me with these words inside), "These are minor miracles; I could do so much more."

13

And Still More

I had another experience with a shiny white vehicle. This time it was a car, or more precisely, a taxi. God again sent an angel just when I needed one.

My husband and I were at the Minneapolis airport getting ready to board a plane for Florida. My husband was attending an industry-wide conference in Florida where he was one of the speakers. I was going along with him.

It was a snowy, muddy, wintery day as only Minnesota can be when we are just on the dividing line between winter and spring. My husband and I drove to the airport and parked our car in the parking lot under the airport.

We had rushed to catch our plane and the plane was just loading passengers. We had found our seats and were adjusting our carry-on luggage overhead, when I heard the Spirit within me say, "Where are you going? I didn't tell you to go. You have work to do that isn't finished."

Well, by now I knew the Holy Spirit's voice well enough to know He was talking to me, but I was challenged. I knew I had heard Him clearly and I did understand something about being tested but I also didn't know how my husband would take it if I got off the plane. Would he be upset with me or would he understand? Actually, I did know. It wouldn't be well-received. (I would feel the same way if the situation was reversed.)

What to do? What to do? And only moments to decide. Would I obey the leading of the Holy Spirit or would I prove that I had more concern for man's opinion of me than God's? I had begun to pray in tongues as soon as I knew what the Lord was saying to me. I knew that—for whatever reason—my answer to this was important.[1]

Finally, without a moment to spare, I whispered to my husband that I had to leave and was going back home. I walked down the plane aisle and back into the airport. Crying a little and praying silently in tongues, I walked down the long corridor and out of the airport to catch a taxi home.

I went out and got in a long line of people waiting to get a taxi. I continued to pray under my breath. It was cold and rainy and gray in the early evening. There was a long line of taxis, too; all were dirty and muddy from the melting snow. One by one, taxis pulled up for the next person in line and, in orderly Minnesota-fashion, we waited our turn.

Suddenly, it was my turn to get into the next taxi. Just then, a shiny-white, perfectly-clean taxi pulled up and inserted itself in line. The driver reached in back and opened the door. I looked up, saw the taxi light on top and got in. The taxi driver asked, "Where to?" and I told him.

We began to converse during the long drive to our outlying suburb. He said he had a 'word of the Lord' for me and began to quote a Bible passage found in Isaiah 43. I have never forgotten and when things are tough, that message continues to give me strength to this day. (And my husband did forgive me but it was a long time before I was invited to go with him on a business trip again.)

> ". . . Do not fear, for I have redeemed you; I have called you by name; you are Mine! When you pass through the waters, I will be with you; and through the rivers, they will not overflow you. When you walk through the fire, you will not be scorched, nor will the flame burn you, for I am the Lord your God, the Holy one of Israel, your Savior . . ."
> (Isaiah 43-1-3)

One day, after I dropped our youngest daughter off at high school, a normal activity since I car-pooled her every weekday, I was driving home not knowing how glad I would be to have that promise as the day wore on. Suddenly I remembered it was National Day of Prayer. I pondered that for a moment and then decided to take a long drive and pray.

I got a 20-oz. Coke (not my wisest move) and headed up Highway 35 toward Duluth. Settling down for a couple hours of driving and praying, I asked the Lord what I should pray about. I thought perhaps it would be something for our nation or our church or something like that because it was the *national* day of prayer. Instead, I was distinctly impressed with these stern words, "Pray for yourself!"

I thought that was strange as I did not know what to pray for myself—everything seemed fine to me. Nonetheless, I started praying in tongues as I drove along, enjoying the nice day. After about an hour, maybe forty-five minutes later, I decided to turn around and head back home—that would fulfill the two hours I had set aside for praying. There was a wayside rest on the right side of the road and I decided to make a quick stop because of all the Coke I had been drinking. Up until that time, I had continued to pray in tongues but with increasing urgency.

I pulled into the wayside rest and noticed that there were quite a few cars around. I decided to wait in my car because the building seemed kind of crowded. Perhaps because of the Coke I drank, or perhaps because the sun was beating down warmly on the windshield of my little car, I grew sleepy.

It was a nice day and after awhile—I don't know how long I slept—I woke up. The other cars had cleared out. I decided to make my stop and then get back on the road toward home. I remember a caretaker could be seen through the glass windows of the wayside rest where he was way down the hill in back, raking leaves or something.

As I approached the building, I noticed a man standing just inside the door. I glanced down at his feet and noticed he was wearing black dress shoes and no socks. Then I noticed he was wearing brand new navy blue denim bib overalls. He had a white dress shirt on, unbuttoned at the neck and was wearing a new straw hat with a piece of wheat coming out of his mouth. He was a caricature of a farmer but nothing added up.

I come from farm stock. I know a farmer when I see one. This one was a fake. Perhaps Mr. Rogers or Captain Kangaroo would have dressed in that get-up but not a genuine farmer. I immediately knew something was wrong and I turned around to walk back to my car, praying silently in tongues.

I didn't know what to do. Nobody else was in the parking lot as I tried to cross over to my car. I could hear the clack of those dress shoes behind me. If I speeded up, the clack speeded up. If I slowed down, the clacking slowed down. I remember thinking; I can't believe this is really happening to me.

I was not quite sure what to do. As I'm praying in tongues and trying to think what to do next, my right hand suddenly shoots up into the air and I call out "Okay!" It was like I was responding to someone a ways down the bike path by the trees—like maybe I'd dropped someone off earlier for a jog and had been waiting in the car to pick him up.

It was the perfect foil, but I certainly didn't devise it. All I know is that the words came out of my mouth. My hand shot up into the air and I waved as if to someone in the distance who was making their way toward me—someone I had promised to pick up. It all came to me in that one moment as my arm was in motion. The clacking heels behind me paused.

Emboldened but knowing my stalker is right behind me, I pretended I didn't know that. I didn't want to hurry him into making a grab for me.

Still praying, and still getting impressions of what to do next, I didn't go directly to the driver's side of the car. Instead I walked behind the car without looking around and unlocked the passenger door and quickly slid in, like whomever the guy was that I was waving to was going to be the driver. Again without turning around, I popped down the lock on my door and leaned back.

I slid my arm over the back of the driver's seat and with the other arm, I kind of half waved to someone or something supposedly over to the right where there was a jogging path and a lot of trees. Then I leaned my head against the back of my seat as though settling in to wait for someone who's finishing their run.

The man behind me is now thoroughly confused. He took some quick steps backward and then I heard quick steps as he started to run for his vehicle. Then he stopped like he was listening and I wondered if he was going to come back toward me. Then I heard quick steps again as he jumped in his vehicle. I heard the door slam and his engine rev as he roared away. I turned around quickly and saw a red van without windows and an emblem or logo of some kind stuck on the metal side of the van.

When I was pretty sure he was gone, I slid over to the driver's side, got behind the wheel and took off; once again, thanking God for His protection and for being able to pray in tongues to get answers about what to do when I didn't know what I ought to do. This did not have a perfect ending though. I think I dropped the ball.

A follow-up to that story (to which I don't think I responded very well) happened a few months later. Returning home after having dropped my daughter off at school that morning, I was driving east on busy highway 694 when I started thinking about what happened that day. I was thinking about what I *should have done* and if I should have called the police to report the driver of the van even though he hadn't done anything.

I was driving along, silently praying in tongues, very relaxed, when I looked in the rearview mirror and there was a red van behind me. I certainly was not expecting any kind of a manifestation of "the man in the red van." I just happened to glance in the rearview mirror as the van pulled up behind me on the freeway, and then quickly passed me. As he did, I saw an emblem on the van and it was skittering back and forth like it was loose.

In a moment, I realized that the driver of the van could tack on the insignia onto the metal side of the van whenever he wanted to be seen as school personnel because the sign swinging back and forth read "School District" with a number after it. I realized it was a perfect camouflage for someone who wanted to seem 'official' at certain times but it could be removed for his own sinister purposes.

In looking back, the Holy Spirit probably wanted me to call in my "non-information" to 911 but I missed my moment to do that. I doubt my encounter with the red van was just coincidental. I regret, even at this late date, not handling that situation better.

In looking back, surely the Lord had me praying in tongues and then brought the red van alongside me for a purpose.

In hindsight, I think I blew it that day.

Chapter 13 Endnotes

[1] Genesis 22; 2 Chronicles 32:20-22

14
Laying on of Hands

Many times I have heard Christians say, "I don't speak in tongues myself but I'm not against tongues. I would be willing to accept them if the Lord gave them to me but, since He's never given them to me, I don't think I'm one who is supposed to have them. But I'm willing if the Lord lays them on me."

But it doesn't work that way. These people are unaware (because it is seldom pointed out in books or church services) that except for the two initial outpourings of the Holy Spirit upon first the Jews and then the Gentiles, the Spirit seldom comes on believers without their invitation. However, with the active participation and desire of the believer, He is *AVAILABLE* to every believer. There is not a two-tier level of Christianity!

However, you aren't forced to participate. As it says in Acts 2, "they," meaning the disciples, began to speak out in tongues—"they" began to speak out loud what they were hearing in their minds—which is the same way we do it today. When we speak in English, we hear (or think) something in our minds and speak it out. Likewise, when we are baptized in the Holy Spirit the words we think or hear are an unfamiliar language given us by the Holy Spirit—the vocalizing (or speaking those words out loud) is done by us with our own mouth.

God's plan—THE PROMISE of the Father—was that He would send the Holy Spirit to *every* believer. The language we receive is how we know we've received the Holy Spirit:

> And it shall come to pass in the last days, says God, that I will pour out of My Spirit on all flesh; Your sons and your daughters shall prophesy, your young men shall see visions, your old men shall dream dreams, and on My menservants and on My maidservants I will pour out My Spirit in those days; and they shall prophesy.
> (Acts 2:17-18)

Not everybody recognizes that being (a) born-again and (b) being baptized in the Holy Spirit are two different things. This is easily pointed out using the Acts 19 example of the Ephesians. They were disciples of Jesus so they were born again but when the Apostle Paul asked them if they had received the Holy Spirit, they didn't even know they were supposed to. They hadn't even received the right water baptism.

The apostle told them two things. First, they had to be baptized properly and, two, they needed to receive the baptism of the Holy Spirit. So, after they were baptized in Jesus' name, Paul laid hands on them and they began to speak in tongues and prophesy. Again, Scripture says "they" began to speak with tongues. The Holy Spirit "baptized" them but He did not "speak" for them.[1]

> And it happened, while Apollos was at Corinth, that Paul, having passed through the upper regions, came to Ephesus. And finding some disciples he said to them, "Did you receive the Holy Spirit when you believed?" So they said to him, "We have not so much as heard whether there is a Holy Spirit." And he said to them, "Into what then were you baptized? So they said, "Into John's baptism." Then Paul said, "John indeed baptized with a baptism of repentance, saying to the people that they should believe on Him who would come after him, that is, on Christ Jesus." When they heard this, they were baptized in the name of the Lord Jesus.[2] And when Paul had laid hands on them, the Holy Spirit came upon them and they spoke with tongues and prophesied. Now the men were about twelve in all." (Acts 19:1-6)

The five examples given in the New Testament of people being born again and then receiving the baptism of the Holy Spirit with the evidence of tongues were given so that no matter what one's situation is, they will know how to proceed in order to become Spirit-filled. They will know when this happens because they will receive the manifestation of tongues as they did in all five examples. For them to be Spirit-filled—and know they have received the

Holy Spirit—is to have a verbal manifestation. This is the full program of God for those who are receiving salvation.

As a result, the Holy Spirit also desires this for us today. The most common way to receive the Holy Spirit is at the time when one accepts Jesus Christ as his Lord and Savior. Helping someone receive the Holy Spirit is usually done through a Spirit-filled believer 'laying on hands' upon a new believer and inviting the Holy Spirit to come upon him/her. This transfers the Holy Spirit from one Christian to another in cases where they have not yet had a verbal manifestation of the Holy Spirit.

John the Baptist declared that all believers are to receive the Holy Spirit:

> John answered, saying to all, "I indeed baptize you with water; but One mightier than I is coming whose sandal strap I am not worthy to loose. He will baptize you with the Holy Spirit and fire. (Luke 3:16)

So even today, the way the Holy Spirit is transferred from one believer to another is through the 'laying on of hands.' One or more believers will lay hands on us, possibly on our head, and pray a simple prayer, inviting Jesus to baptize us with His Holy Spirit.

We, in turn, respond by praying a simple prayer asking God for the Holy Spirit. As we do, we will begin to softly hear words in our mind (words that are of a different language and don't make sense to us). To put those words (almost just thoughts) in our

106

mind is the job of the Holy Spirit. Our job is to then speak these words out loud just as we would do in English (or whatever our native language is).

It is that simple! Occasionally, it will happen without the laying on of hands as it did for me. I had never heard whether there was a Holy Spirit but when I put my faith in Jesus and was born again, I also received a song in my heart which I now know is called 'singing in the Spirit.' It was fun and it takes away all gray moods and discouragement. I could then pray in words once I learned about the baptism of the Holy Spirit.

But generally it is through the laying on of hands that 'being baptized in the Spirit' happens—as it did with the early Church after the first two initial outpourings, one for the Jews and one for the Gentiles—and that is how it is intended to work in today's Church, too.

Receiving the gift of tongues is the rightful gift for one who is born again. Another time when we are very open to receiving the baptism of the Holy Spirit with the sign of tongues is just after we are baptized in water. In fact, that's when Jesus received His empowerment by the Holy Spirit.

> Now when all the people were baptized, Jesus was also baptized, and while He was praying, heaven was opened, and the Holy Spirit descended upon Him in bodily form like a dove, and a voice came out of heaven, "You are My beloved Son, In You I am

well-pleased." (Luke 3:21, 22)

Apparently in the New Testament times, *'laying on of hands'* was such a well known concept that no one felt the need to explain it. This is easy to understand because the Old Testament Jew often used the laying on of hands. One example would be to impart a blessing as the male head of the household does each Sabbath evening before partaking of the special meal. The blessing is pronounced on the female head of the household and all of their children.

In the five examples given in the New Testament of receiving the Holy Spirit, I would discover that 'laying on of hands' was considered an elementary teaching and the usual way for this transfer taking place. This concept is one of the building blocks one needs to understand in order to go on to Christian maturity:

> Therefore, leaving the discussion of the elementary principles of Christ, let us go on to perfection, not laying again the foundation of repentance from dead works and of faith toward God, of the doctrine of baptisms, of laying on of hands, of resurrection of the dead, and of eternal judgment. And this we will do if God permits." (Hebrews 6:1-3)

When one joins a Bible study today, *laying on of hands* is not often discussed. Yet, in Scripture, there are certain times when the laying on of hands *is talked about* and we would do well to gain an understanding of the matter by studying these examples.

Chapter 14 Endnotes

---

[1] Acts 19:1-6
[2] Acts 2:38

15

Learning How

The Bible says that God is looking for those who will worship Him "in Spirit and in truth." It was for that reason that the whole package of God given by the Apostle Peter—including the manifestation of the gift of tongues by the Holy Spirit—was held in high esteem by the early Church.

In fact, the whole 1-2-3 plan of God was considered absolutely necessary before one could be considered fully equipped as a Christian; i.e., repentance, water baptism *and the gift of the Holy Spirit.*

> Then Peter said to them, "Repent, and let every one of you be baptized in the name of Jesus Christ for the remission of sins; and you shall receive the gift of the Holy Spirit. For the promise [of receiving the Spirit] is to you and to your children, and to all who are afar off, as many as the Lord our God will call. (Acts 2:38, 39, emphasis added)

They made sure each one who was born again also spoke in tongues. The following examples are given so that every Christian may know that the gift of the Holy Spirit is intended for every one of them, as many as have believed. God does not desire for them to miss out.

When it was supposed that a believer or a group of believers had been born again but had not yet manifested the outward evidence of the indwelling Holy Spirit—i.e., received an out-loud, verbal manifestation of the Holy Spirit—one or more followers of Christ were sent to 'lay on hands' and pray for that person to receive the transference of the Holy Spirit.

It was considered an unfinished initiation into Christianity until this happened. In close study of the examples given in the New Testament, I had to draw the conclusion that, yes, all *can* speak in tongues once they have been born again because that is the way the early Church looked at it.

In this way, the early Church made sure that, without fail, everyone was empowered with the Holy Spirit. Praying in tongues is like the prelude to the other gifts of the Holy Spirit, the more likely it is that one will prophesy or impart healing to another or have a "word" of wisdom or knowledge to share with their seeking brother or sister. That is why the early Church was so powerful.

That is why the question is often asked, "But do all speak in tongues?" The answer is that all born again believers *can speak in tongues*—but do all believers? No, they have been taught that tongues are only for some and so when they do not manifest the gift of the Holy Spirit when they are born again they accept that version as the will of God. Yet in studying the New Testament, it becomes obvious *that all born again believers have tongues,* they just do not know how to activate them.

The Apostle Paul, in I Corinthians 14, said, "I speak in tongues more than you all." He also said in the same chapter, "I wish you all spoke in tongues;" and earlier in the same chapter he wrote that prophecy was a greater gift than tongues, *unless one's gift of tongues is accompanied by the gift of interpretation: "Therefore let him who speaks in a tongue pray that he may interpret: "Therefore let him who speaks in a tongue pray that he may interpret."* [1]

So we discover that there is a protocol to speaking in tongues, God desires that *all* pray in tongues but He also wants them to pray in English (or whatever their native language is). Although, praying in tongues is praying perfectly because it is the Spirit of Jesus (the Spirit of God) who is giving us the words which we then verbalize out loud, it does not negate praying in one's own native *learned* language:

> "What is the conclusion then? I will pray with the spirit, and I will also pray with the understanding, I will sing with the spirit, and I will also sing with the understanding."
> (I Corinthians 14:15)

There are five examples given in the New Testament of believers proving that the Holy Spirit has come upon them by receiving the out-loud prayer language of the Holy Spirit. In fact, it is not often pointed out that in only two of the five illustrations given as examples of the coming of the Holy Spirit upon believers did the initial outpouring happen to them automatically *or sovereignly.*

The first two examples were the *initial* outpouring on the Jews and the initial outpouring on the Gentiles at Cornelius' house. In the remaining three examples, the Holy Spirit did not come unless He was given an invitation. Even then it was not an outpouring as at the first; it was when the apostles figured out that something was missing in the Christian walk of a new group (or individual). When it was determined that they had not received the Holy Spirit, it was administered through the 'laying on of hands.'

How did they figure out that these new *already-believers* had not yet received the Holy Spirit? It was because they had not yet heard them speak in tongues and/or prophesy!

Why this is not discussed more is unfortunate because Christians are left to believe that they personally have nothing to do with whether or not they receive the Holy Spirit; or—worse yet—that they have been passed over and the Holy Spirit is not willing to come to them. In fact, the failure is always man's because man has failed to teach that the Holy Spirit is generally given—transferred—through the laying on of hands *not sovereignly,* although this can happen.

Admittedly, my experience was a little different yet. I was a little lost soul in no man's land—at least it seemed that way spiritually. There was no one to initiate me into the experience and I was young and inexperienced so the Holy Spirit had little difficulty breaking through. I had no sophisticated barriers that had to be broken down in order to receive my joyful little songs.

Though there are many examples in the Old Testament of the Holy Spirit coming upon a specific individual for a specific task, this is not what generally happens. To demonstrate, the Bible gives us five different examples of the Holy Spirit coming on people with the outward proof of His indwelling being speaking in tongues. The tongues allow people to know if they have received or not.

In every one of the following examples except the two initial outpourings on the Jew and the Gentile, the Holy Spirit was given—not automatically—but with the laying on of hands:

1. The original outpouring of the Holy Spirit on the Jews (Acts 2).
2. The original outpouring of the Holy Spirit on the Gentiles (Acts 10).
3. The Samaritans already were believers and been baptized in water in the name of Jesus Christ but they had not yet received the Holy Spirit. Then the Apostle Paul laid hands on them and they received the Holy Spirit (Acts 8).
4. The Apostle Paul believed but had not yet been water-baptized nor had he received the Holy Spirit (Acts 9). Later he said, "I wish you all spoke in tongues,"[2] and "I

thank God I speak in tongues more than you all."[3]

5. The Ephesians were believers in Jesus but had only received John's baptism. The apostle said they must receive Jesus' baptism as well, so he commanded them to be re-baptized into Jesus' name for the remission of sin. So he laid hands on them and they received the gift of the Holy Spirit with evidence of tongues. (Acts 19).

In the original outpouring of the Holy Spirit upon the Jews (also the original outpouring on the Gentiles), the Holy Spirit came sovereignly and automatically upon them. These two outpourings happened without the laying on of hands. Still, they were commanded to be baptized into the name of Jesus Christ for the remission of sin, with the word 'remission' meaning to have one's sin nature removed.[4]

This transference happened fifty days after Jesus ascended into heaven and sent the Holy Spirit as promised. It happened on a day specifically set aside by God thousands of years earlier and which we call "Pentecost." This was the sovereign move of God for which 120 believers had been praying in the Upper Room. All other examples where the Holy Spirit was received, He was transferred from one believer to another using the method of laying on of hands.

"And leaving the discussion of the elementary principles of Christ, let us go on to perfection, not laying again the foundation of repentance from dead works and of faith toward God, of the doctrine of baptisms, of laying on of hands, of resurrection of the dead, and of eternal judgment. And this we will do if God permits." (Hebrews 6:1-3)

"And when the day of Pentecost had fully come, they were all with one accord in one place. And suddenly there came a sound from heaven, as of a rushing mighty wind, and it filled the whole house where they were sitting. And there appeared to them divided tongues, as of fire, and one sat upon each of them. And they were all filled with the Holy Spirit and began to speak with other tongues, as the Spirit gave them utterance." (Acts 2:1-4)

"Peter said [to the distraught Jews who had just murdered their Messiah], 'Repent, and let every one of you be baptized in the name of Jesus Christ for the remission of sins; and you shall receive the gift of the Holy Spirit. For the promise is to you and to your children, and to all who are afar off, as many as the Lord our God will call." (Acts 2:38, 39)

In the second example the Holy Spirit *automatically* came upon the Gentiles, but it was also only one time. A pious Roman centurion named Cornelius was zealous for God and did many good works that benefited the Jews and honored God. God saw his sincerity and gave Cornelius' a vision instructing him to send for the apostle Peter.

Meanwhile, Peter was given a vision showing him to no longer call the Gentiles 'unclean,' but to go and preach the gospel to them. When Cornelius' men showed up at his door, Peter left with them. While he was still preaching the gospel to them, the Holy Spirit fell on those that believed *without the laying on of hands* and they all spoke in tongues. Peter then baptized them in water, seeing as how God had accepted them the same as he had accepted the Jews:

> While Peter was still speaking these words, the Holy Spirit fell upon all those who heard the word. And those of the circumcision who believed were astonished, as many as came with Peter, because the gift of the Holy Spirit had been poured out on the Gentiles also. For they heard them speak with tongues and magnify God. Then Peter answered, "Can anyone forbid water, that these should not be baptized who have received the Holy Spirit just as we have? And he commanded them to be baptized in the name of the Lord...." (Acts 10:44-48)

The next three examples were ingeniously chosen by the Holy Spirit to showcase all the likely combinations of people seeking the infilling of the Holy Spirit. be included in the Bible to showcase answers to three questions that believers might possibly wonder about as they seek to receive the 'baptism of the Holy Spirit.'

The first example happened to the Samaritans. This again was slightly different from the other examples. It answers the question of whether one needs to pray in tongues as a sign that one has received the Holy Spirit. The Samaritans had believed, repented, been baptized in water but had not yet received the Holy Spirit.

The apostles Peter and John were sent to lay on hands on the new Samaritan believers because although they had repented and been baptized in water, there was no evidence that the Holy Spirit had yet fallen on them. Seeing this, apostles laid hands on them and transferred the Holy Spirit to these believers. We know Simon the sorcerer saw something extraordinary happen to them when that happened because he offered money to the apostles to buy that 'manifestation' from them:

> "Now when the apostles who were at Jerusalem heard that Samaria had received the word of God, they sent Peter and John to them, who, when they had come down, prayed for them that they might receive the Holy Spirit, for as yet He had fallen upon none of them. They had only been baptized into the name of the Lord Jesus. Then they laid hands on them and they received the Holy Spirit. Now when Simon saw that the Spirit was bestowed through the laying on of the apostles' hands, he offered them money." (Acts 8:14-18)

The fourth example was when the Lord told the prophet Ananias to go to Straight Street.' There he would find a man notorious for abusing and throwing Christians into prison. He was to lay on hands[5] on Saul so that his sight might be restored. Ananias was understandably afraid but the Lord explained that He was now a follower of the very cause he'd tried to destroy

> "And the Lord said to him, "Arise and go to the street called Straight, and inquire at the house of Judas for one called Saul of Tarsus coming in and putting his hand on him, so that he might receive his sight.".....and laying his hands on him he said, "Brother Saul, the Lord Jesus, who appeared to you on the road as you came, has sent me that you may receive your sight and be filled with the Holy Spirit." Immediately there fell from his eyes something like scales, and he received his sight at once; and he arose and was baptized." (Acts 9:11-18)

In another example, the Ephesians were already believers but they had not yet been baptized into the name of Jesus Christ. They had received only John's baptism. That baptism didn't count for they were told they must be baptized into the name of Jesus Christ for the remission of their sins. So he laid hands on them and they received the gift of the Holy Spirit. How did they know? They spoke in tongues!

> "Then Paul said, "John indeed baptized with a baptism of repentance, saying to the

people that they should believe on Him who would come after him, that is, on Christ Jesus." When they heard this, they were baptized in the name of the Lord Jesus. And when Paul had laid hands on them the Holy Spirit came upon them, and they spoke with tongues and prophesied." (Acts 19:1-6)

So the early Church was more diligent than the churches in our day. They left nothing to chance. They knew how important the Holy Spirit was in the life of a believer. They remembered the difference He had made in their own lives and how necessary receiving the Holy Spirit is for every Christian.

It is often thought today that one has a choice of whether to be baptized with the Holy Spirit or not. We think we have a choice but that is not biblical Christianity. This is a good time to re-read the Book of Acts so we can be reminded of what genuine Christianity ought to look like. The Book of Acts is our instruction manual for living the Christian life:

"And, [Jesus] being assembled together with them, commanded them that they should not depart from Jerusalem, but wait for the promise of the Father, which, saith he, ye have heard of me. For John truly baptized with water; but ye shall be baptized with the Holy Ghost not many days hence."
(Acts 1:4-5)

"For the promise is unto you, and to your children, and to all that are afar off, even as many as the Lord our God shall call."

121

(Acts 2:39)

"The Promise" was God's century's long planning and teaching about the Holy Spirit and the fact that He would one day come on ordinary believers—not just the priests, prophets and kings!

As long as the Holy Spirit was welcomed in the Church, the Church prospered and remained strong.

Chapter 15 Endnotes

---

[1] I Corinthians 14:5, 13, 18
[2] I Corinthians 14:5
[3] I Corinthians 14:18
[4] See Water Baptism: God's Test,
www.judymcclary.com)
[5] Acts 9:12, 17

16

Empowered by the Spirit

The Holy Spirit's purpose was not to glorify Himself. It was to glorify Jesus. This distinction is very important. Power is manifested in a church service when the Holy Spirit is welcomed and allowed to exalt the name of Jesus.

> He [the Holy Spirit] will glorify Me, for He will take of what is Mine and declare it to you." (John 16:12-14)

I knew Jesus had put away equality with God to identify with mankind and yet I was shocked to discover that He continued to be dependent on the Holy Spirit even after His death! If this is correct, it is almost too much to take in because we, too, are dependent on the Holy Spirit. The Bible says even after Jesus' resurrection, He gave instruction to His disciples through the power of the Holy Spirit.

> The former account I made, O Theophilus, of all that Jesus began both to do and teach, until the day in which He was taken up, after He *through the Holy Spirit* had given commandment to the apostles whom He had

chosen." (Acts 1:1-2, italics added)

Until I discovered this in Scripture, I had not realized how thoroughly and completely Jesus identified with mankind. The question I had was why did Jesus rely on the Holy Spirit after His death, burial and resurrection? I wondered why He didn't just teach from His position as the glorified Son of God? He had already fulfilled His time as a man by coming to earth and dying on the Cross—the Atonement for mankind's sin had already been made. Why was He *still walking in the Spirit* instead of walking in the power and glory He had before He came to earth?

And, yet, should I have been surprised? I knew that Jesus emptied Himself of all that was God when He came down to earth as a baby born in Bethlehem. This is general knowledge among the church crowd because the Bible states it so explicitly:

> . . . Christ Jesus, who, although He existed
> in the form of God, did not regard equality
> with God a thing to be grasped, but emptied
> Himself, taking the form of a bond servant,
> and being made in the likeness of men.
> (Philippians 2:5-7 NASB)

I knew that the Spirit of God came upon Jesus as He came up out of the Jordan River after His baptism. In fact, a dove symbolizing the Holy Spirit descended upon Him and the voice of God the Father rang out—"*This is My beloved Son in whom I am well-pleased*!" So there is no doubt that He was Spirit-filled. But why did He continue to 'walk in the

126

Spirit,' when He could have walked in His own power as the resurrected Son of God?

We are told that Jesus—filled with the Holy Spirit—was driven out in the wilderness for a forty days confrontation with Satan. Again, He fulfilled perfectly the plan of God. He was victorious over all that Satan threw against Him during those days— even while being on a starvation fast during those forty days.

And of course the Bible states that when Jesus returned to Galilee, after His encounter with Satan, it was *in the power of the Holy Spirit.*[1] Clearly a victory had been won and Jesus' Holy Spirit experience continued throughout His three-year ministry.

It is also clearly set forth that Jesus did not perform any of His miracles until after He returned from the wilderness experience with Satan. At that time, He turned water into wine at the wedding at Cana—Scripture clearly designated it as His first miracle so that the silly writings circulating declaring that He performed miracles before His empowerment by the Holy Spirit were just that—silly.[2] To remove all doubt about that, His second miracle is also designated.[3]

In fact, most know that the Holy Spirit empowered Jesus *during all His years of ministry* but the fact that He continued to operate in the power of the Holy Spirit after His resurrection is not generally discussed. My question—still unanswered—is could Jesus *really have gone that far in identifying with mankind* that He chose to remain in the same state as we—a member of the converted human race empowered by the Holy Spirit—after His resurrection?

If not, WHY did He continue to minister through the Holy Spirit even after His death and resurrection? The Ascension had already occurred when the Book of Acts begins. He had already returned to the Father and deposited His holy blood in the heavenly tabernacle. He had resumed His rightful position as God and Son of God.

It was *after His glorification* that the Bible says He gave instruction to His disciples through the Holy Spirit. Was He continuing to walk in the power of the Holy Spirit just as He had while on earth? Is that what He is also doing in heaven today?

> "The former account I made, O Theophilus, of all that Jesus began both to do and teach, until the day in which He was taken up, after He <u>through the Holy Spirit</u> had given commandments to the apostles whom He had chosen, to whom He also presented Himself alive after His suffering by many infallible proofs, being seen by them during forty days and speaking of the things pertaining to the kingdom of God." (Acts 1:1-3, emph.added)

We need to fall on our faces and repent that we, as a Church, have been very cavalier about accepting the ministry of the Holy Spirit. If even Jesus accepted the ministry of the Holy Spirit so completely, shouldn't we? On the Day of Pentecost, the Jews were accused of being *stiff-necked* regarding the Holy Spirit. We have been no better.

God sent His Holy Spirit here to earth to assist us in our Christian walk after sending His own Son to model the walk in the Spirit. Jesus Christ had been sent as the supreme sacrifice, coming to earth as a human baby and living out His brief life for this purpose – to show future believers how to walk in the Spirit. Most have not yet begun to comprehend His sacrifice.

When we study how intensely active the Holy Spirit was in the Old Testament and then look at the very many miracles Jesus did in the New Testament, we can begin to understand just a little of the Spirit's intended purpose in our own life. The fact that the Holy Spirit of God is now indwelling us in the same way that He once indwelt Jesus should give us pause—how have we welcomed God's Holy Spirit and what are we doing about it?

In the Book of Mark alone, 209 of the 661 verses deal with miracles performed by Jesus Christ for the purpose of alleviating the suffering of mankind. The reason for those miracles—besides compassion for the suffering of mankind because of Satan's evil works—was to give them the faith to believe that He was the Messiah, sent to be their Savior. They needed to believe that His blood, shed on Calvary, would pay their load of sin and bring reconciliation with God and forgiveness of sin—if they believed.

So Jesus' miracles not only healed people, they helped them believe. Jesus wanted them to receive His Holy Spirit so they could do the same for beleaguered mankind. He set an example for us on why we should welcome the Holy Spirit in our life as we see the part the Holy Spirit played in His life. For as He went about preaching and performing miracles, we are to take His example and do the same— proclaiming Jesus' name as *the only way* to be saved *because:*

> He who has the Son has eternal life; he who does not have the Son of God does not have life. (I John 5:12)

When we look at His last instructions at the end of the Book of Mark, we see that it was this same pattern that He wanted His disciples (us) to follow:

> So then, when the Lord Jesus had spoken to them, He was received up into heaven and sat down at the right hand of God. And they went out and preached everywhere, while the Lord worked with them, and confirmed the word by the signs that followed.
> (Mark 16:19-20 NASB)

It is good for us to know what kind of miracles Jesus performed. That way, we have some idea of what the average believer of today might expect to perform when they are bold enough to stand against current false teaching that the time of the Holy Spirit is past. For Jesus said we would do greater works than He.

The following list is not exhaustive but if we, too, are to walk in signs and wonders such as those performed by Jesus, we can expect to see some of these things manifested by the Holy Spirit in our own lives as we lay on hands on the sick and people are healed and set free. Each generation needs to see the power of God. All these miracles and more were performed by the hand of Jesus *through the same empowerment of the Holy Spirit that we are given through the Laying on of Hands.*

- Jesus healed a deaf mute (Mt.9:32-34)
- He sent Peter to take a coin from the mouth of the first fish to caught to pay both His and Peter's taxes (Mt.17:24-27)
- Healed a man of demonic possession (Mk.1:21-28)
- Healed Peter's mother-in-law of a fever (Mk.1:29-31)
- Healed leprosy (Mk.1:40-45)
- Healed paralysis (Mk.2:1-12)
- Healed a withered hand (Mk.3:1-6)
- Stilled the storm (Mk.4:35-41)
- Healed an issue of blood (Mk.5:25-34)
- Raised the dead (Mk.5:35-43; Lk.7:11-15; Jn.11:1-44)
- Walked on water (Mk.6:45-52)
- Fed the five thousand (Mk.6:30-44)
- Fed the four thousand (Mk.8:1-10)
- Healed blindness (Mk.8:22-26)
- Healed epilepsy (Mk.9:14-29)
- Cursed the fig tree and made it wither overnight (Mk.11:12-14, 20-35)

- Brought in a huge catch of fish for His disciples (Lk.5:1-11; Jn.21:1-14)
- Healed a deformed hand (Lk.13:10-17)
- Healed dropsy (Lk.14:1-6)
- Restored an ear that had been chopped off by Peter's sword (Lk. 22:50, 51)
- He rose into the clouds and ascended back into heaven with five hundred witnesses who later mouthed it abroad, (Lk. 24:50-53; Acts 1:9)
- His first-ever miracle was turning water into wine (Jn.2:1-11)

Over the centuries, Christians (people still following the Book of Acts habit of requiring believers to 'repent, be baptized into the name of Jesus Christ for the remission of sins and receive the gift of the Holy Spirit)' have caused a mighty big problem for those in churches who have been taught by liberal theologians to ignore the Book of Acts.

More than a hundred years ago, once-well-known, liberal New Testament Bible scholar Adolf von Harnack wrote a book called *What is Christianity* which influenced many in his generation. In it, he wrote of his disapproval of the idea of miracles. He said miracles were not possible because they interrupted God's assigned laws of nature. He spoke this, apparently without realizing that *that is exactly what miracles are supposed to do!*

> "We are firmly convinced that what happens in space and time is subject to the general laws of motion, and that in this sense, as an

> interruption of the order of Nature, there can
> be no such things as 'miracles.'[4]

Being distrustful of the Spirit is not a new phenomenon in the twenty-first century. The first Christian martyr, Stephen, was "full of faith and power" and he did miracles and signs and wonders which stirred up the Pharisees against him. They brought in false witnesses against him but Stephen was not intimidated. He said.

> "You stiff-necked and uncircumcised in
> heart and ears! You always resist the Holy
> Spirit; as your fathers did, so do you."
> (Acts 8:51)

And, indeed, two thousand years later miracles are continuing to happen in places where faith is present—although not in dead churches where there is no faith. So, yes, there are churches today that are not walking in signs and miracles and have refused entrance of the Holy Spirit but who still wish to keep the name "church" on their letterhead.

To keep from looking silly and as if they are only facsimiles of the genuine church, they support godless teaching such as Martin Luther's statement that the Age of the Spirit has ceased. God knew this would happen. His Holy Spirit prophesied this would be very much the condition of the Church just before the Second Coming of Jesus:

> But realize this, that in the last days difficult
> times will come, for men will be lovers of
> self, lovers of money, boastful, arrogant,

revilers, disobedient to parents, ungrateful, unholy, unloving, irreconcilable, malicious gossips, without self-control, brutal, haters of good, treacherous, reckless, conceited, lovers of pleasure rather than lovers of God, *hold to a form of godliness, although they have denied its power;* Avoid such men as these.

(2 Timothy 3:1-5 NASB, emphasis added)

The Bible says we are to skirt a big path around those that have the *appearance of godliness,* but deny *the Holy Spirit's power.*

Chapter 16 Endnotes

[1] Luke 3:22-23

[2] John 2:11

[3] John 4:54

[4] *What is Christianity* by Adolf von Harnack. 28-29. (New York: Putnam, 1901). (Stein, 19.)

17

The Rest of the Story

Perhaps enough proof has been given that the Holy Spirit is alive and active today that I can conclude this book by telling *the rest of the story* of the shiny white monster pickup truck.

I shared part of the story earlier. I told of the day when the *God-in-me—the Holy Spirit—h*ad to produce a white shiny pickup truck to rescue me in the wilds of northern Minnesota. At that time, I told only half the story because I thought it might be too much to relate for people who don't know me. I no longer believe that to be the case.

So now that our *expectancy* has been raised, I will return to the story and tell how the Holy Spirit built a road for me to escape my would-be persecutor. I had been forced to follow a beat-up old red pickup truck for a mile or so. The driver kept going slower and slower. I was forced to stay behind him because on one side of the narrow dirt road there was a forest and on the other side, swamp water came up to the edge and I couldn't get around him or turn back.

In an earlier chapter, I wrote about the white and shiny new, dust-free monster-size pickup truck that had suddenly appeared in my rearview mirror. But I didn't tell you what happened just before I ended up in that predicament which I could have avoided if I had blindly followed the Holy Spirit's direction so it really was my own fault that I ended up in that predicament but He rescued me anyway.

The part of the story I left out was how I ended up on an old dirt road in the first place. However, I had not a clue of how to get where I wanted to go. I had traveled north about five hours from my home city. I was headed to the camp where I planned to stay a few days and do some writing. When I arrived in a not-so little tourist town with a great big lake as you enter town, I wanted to get on the smaller road that then leads to a smaller-yet side road and follow it on to the camp. Remember, I am directionally-challenged.

A road crew had been doing the perennial Minnesota-thing of fixing roads all summer long. As a result, the road I ordinarily took through town was torn up. I ended up on a road headed out of town in a slightly different direction than the usual route although it seemed like it would end up close to where I wanted to go. On my GPS was an arrow pointing to a tiny little town which was twenty-five miles further down the road. I thought I would turn off when I got there and ask directions. The road suggested by my GPS was a nice blacktop road and so I took it.

After I had traveled perhaps twenty miles, my GPS showed that I had to turn onto a dirt road. I did this, following the signs closely until I arrived at the little town closest to the area. I thought someone there would be able to give me more exact directions. I stopped at a place where there was someone in town who seemed reliable and got more exact directions. I started out but, because the roads were so poorly marked, I got mixed up and couldn't find the exact road I was looking for.

Not knowing where to go next and because the sun was starting to go down, I was beginning to worry about being in that area alone after dark. There was water on both sides of the dirt roads and it was getting more and more unfamiliar and, because of the tall trees, I was having trouble getting accurate satellite readings on my GPS.

I used my cell phone and tried to call ahead. Someone answered the phone but because I didn't know exactly where I was at, they couldn't really help me. After giving me a couple of general suggestions, I was on my own.

By this time, dear readers, I don't need to remind you that I was praying madly in tongues because I had no more English words of instruction for telling God how to save me(!) so I was happy to be able to pray in tongues; normal prayer was not good enough. My GPS was still plugged in but it seemed completely confused what with the name of some unfamiliar-sounding avenue showing up as a place I was to make a left-hand turn. (This was before I met the man and the pickup which I would meet later when I didn't follow my GPS's directions.)

I kept driving and suddenly up ahead was what looked like a street sign in an urban residential area rather than the usual rural road sign. But there it was. My GPS said to turn left. It looked suspicious to me. I thought perhaps my GPS wasn't connecting with a satellite because of all the trees.

Even so, I knew I was lost and the GPS was giving me directions and this street sign was on the GPS. I turned left at the official-looking, green avenue sign affixed to the side of the road. As I turned onto the path, road, avenue or whatever, it seemed to be no more than a path when I got on it. I noticed that the corn was taller on both sides of the car than any corn I'd ever seen—it seemed at least ten feet tall.

The road looked like it had just been built. The dirt was smooth but it was dark like dirt freshly turned over. I wasn't very far into the road when I wanted to turn around and go back the way I had come but the road wasn't wide enough and besides, I was afraid I'd get stuck because the road was only a little over a car-width wide. I knew if I got stuck nobody might find me until harvest time because even if I walked out, where would I go to find someone—and my phone wasn't working anymore.

Believe me, I kept praying. Finally, I came to the end of the road or street or whatever it was. My GPS had sent me there and had listed this newly-made path through someone's cornfield as a legitimate street. Now it was giving directions to turn right or left. Didn't matter, I didn't trust it anymore.

So instead of turning the direction it told me, I turned in the opposite direction. I didn't trust it anymore because of the terrible predicament I believed it had just gotten me into—and so I turned in the opposite direction.

Only later would I realize that the GPS was not malfunctioning as much as it was God-functioning. The new avenue God had taken me through was so that I could escape a potential attacker up ahead. But now, I had chosen to go in the opposite way the GPS was telling me to go. I drove up a little incline to get out of the cornfield and back onto the public road. After driving a mile to two, I ended up behind a disreputable-looking driver in a beat up, red pickup truck. And you already know the rest of the story!

As I tried to figure out what to do, of course, I was praying violently in tongues. When I thought I was about to be forced off the road, up behind me came the shiny clean, chrome-trimmed white monster-sized pickup truck. I looked in the side mirror of the pickup ahead of me and saw the shocked and terrified look on the face of my would-be assailant. He sped up and soon was lost from sight.

I thank God for the ability to pray in a supernatural language that I never learned. If I had been praying in English—even if I had thought of asking God to send an angel and a big white pickup truck to scare off my adversary—I would never have had the boldness to ask for anything as audacious as a newly-built road through a farmer's cornfield! Even now I shiver at the thought of what might have happened if the Holy Spirit had not intervened.

Yet even when I failed to trust God's first escape plan that He set up for me when He told me to turn left after driving through the brand-new pathway He'd put together through the cornfield, He was kind enough to send plan B. I remember saying to the Holy Spirit that day, "God, this is over the top!"

He responded by telling me that He had the capability of doing so much more for His children; that He was only limited by their faith.

I thought back to the ten plagues He had sent to free the Israelites in Egypt and how He held back the waters of the Red Sea and brought forth water out of a rock in the desert for two million people to drink; and I thought, "*He's right.*"

The Bible verse that states "faith cometh by hearing God's Word" came to mind, and I made plans to redouble my Bible reading.

The End

Appendix i

Back to Faith Alone

God is not willing that any should perish. What He's done for one, He will do for another; He is not a respecter of persons.

Jesus Christ, as our Redeemer, is coming soon. At that time, those who have placed their faith in Him but have not yet died and ascended to heaven will rise to meet Him in the air. In order to be accepted in this number, Jesus described an experience we must have. His terminology for it was "born again:"

> Jesus said: Verily, verily, I say unto thee, "Except a man be born again, he cannot see the kingdom of God...Marvel not that I said unto thee, Ye must be born again.
> (John 3:3, 7)

> Jesus said: I am the way, the truth, and the life. No one comes to the Father except through Me. (John 14:6)

> All that the Father gives Me will come to Me, and the one who comes to Me I will by no means cast out. (John 6:37)

For all have sinned and fall short of the glory of God, being justified freely by His grace through the redemption that is in Christ Jesus, whom God set forth as a propitiation by His blood, though faith, to demonstrate His righteousness, because in His forbearance God had passed over the sins that were previously committed, to demonstrate at the present time His righteousness, that He might be just and the justifier of the one who has faith in Jesus. (Romans 3:23-26)

If you confess with your mouth the Lord Jesus and believe in your heart that God has raised Him from the dead, you will be saved. For with the heart one believes unto righteousness, and with the mouth confession is made unto salvation ...Whoever believes on Him will not be put to shame ... For "whoever calls upon the name of the LORD shall be saved." (Romans 10:9-11-13)

God made it simple for us because He is not willing that any should perish.[1] If you want eternal life and believe that Jesus is God's Son and that He died, was buried, and resurrected, tell Him. Pray your own prayer, or say something like this:

God, I believe that Jesus is Your only begotten Son and that He died, was buried, and that He rose again. I choose to make Jesus the Lord of my life. Come into my

144

heart, Lord Jesus. Amen.

Now, be baptized in water! Make Jesus truly Lord of your life. The Bible says, "Or do you not know that as many of us as were baptized into Christ Jesus were baptized in His death ... For IF we have been united together in the likeness of His death, certainly we shall be *in the likeness of His* resurrection," (Rom.6:3-5).

> "Or do you not know that as many of us as were baptized into Christ Jesus were baptized into His death? Therefore we were buried with Him through baptism into death, that just as Christ was raised from the dead by the glory of the Father; even so we also should walk in newness of life. For if we have been united together in the likeness of His death, certainly we also shall be *in the likeness of His* resurrection," (Romans 5:3-5)

In other words, water baptism is important. IF we die with Christ, we will also *rise to newness of life.* It is an action we take to show our faith in Christ's finished work of the cross on our behalf. Just as Abraham the Old Testament patriarch of our faith submitted to the ritual of circumcision to show his faith was genuine (at the same time, giving his descendants a ritual whereby they could also be included in God's covenant), we submit to water baptism—as a *type of spiritual circumcision.* (See Col.2:11-12.)

145

Being baptized into the name of Jesus Christ for the remission of sin is not an optional action. You are commanded to *"repent, be baptized into the name of Jesus Christ for the remission of sin,"* Acts 2:38,*"and you will receive the gift of the Holy Spirit."* While it does not save us (Christ's shed blood has already provided salvation) the Bible is quite clear that there is an "IF" included. IF we are united with Christ in water baptism, we will also rise to newness of life, (Rom.6:4).

What if we were baptized as infants? We are to be rebaptized! If we have been baptized into something other than Jesus' name, we are to be re-baptized. Rebaptism is not a problem for God. In the early Church, rebaptism was dealt with as an unimportant issue. The new disciples were to receive the Bible baptism of believers, that of the baptism into the name of Jesus (See Acts 19:1-6.), even if they'd been baptized into something else first.

Tell your priest or pastor that you want to take part in biblical water baptism. This means an after conversion/full immersion baptism into the name of Jesus, as in the Book of Acts. The Bible is very clear about this. It says "let every one of you" take part in this baptism. It is for every believer. It is the way of the Cross.

God's provision for us was never to change until the second coming of Christ and includes receiving the gift of the Holy Spirit. In all the examples given in the Book of Acts after the Day of Pentecost, if the Holy Spirit was not openly and audibly manifested, before or after water baptism, disciples were dispatched to lay hands on them and bring them into that experience.

Neither water baptism nor receiving the Holy Spirit was taken casually.[2] If your pastor or priest won't baptize you (or rebaptize you if you've only received infant baptism) after you believe, God will help you find one that will, for this is the full program of God. Baptism doesn't save you, but it shows God that your faith is genuine.

> Repent, and let every one of you be baptized
> in the name of Jesus Christ for the remission
> of sins; and you shall receive the gift of the
> Holy Spirit. For the promise is to you and to
> your children, and to all who are afar off, as
> many as the Lord our God will call.
> (Acts 2:38-39)

Reflect and decide now. The Bible says that faith without actions is dead.[3] Jesus commanded baptism.[4] Be baptized in water *and in the Spirit* ....

Appendix i Endnotes

---

[1]   2 Peter 3:9

[2] Samaritans—Acts 8:1, 17; Ethiopian eunuch—Acts
8:26–38; Saul/Paul's conversion—Acts 9:1–19;
Cornelius's household—Acts 10:1–48; Lydia's
household—Acts 16:11–15; Philippians jailer's
household—Acts 16:25–34; the Ephesians—Acts 19:1–10

[3]   James 2:17

[4]   Matthew 28:19; Mark 16:16

AUTHOR'S PAGE

Judith McClary has had a deep interest in Christian spirituality and theology all of her adult life. It has been her joy to study Scripture in formal and informal Christian settings and in daily personal study. She has taught Sunday school, led care groups, and written Bible study guides and Christian education curricula for people of all ages in service of her local church.

To contact the author or invite her to speak at your prayer group or meeting; e-mail or visit her website:

www.judymcclary.com
judymcclary@gmail.com

Believer Baptism testimonies. The author would love to have your testimony of your Acts 2:38 water baptism for possible inclusion in a future book on after-conversion, full-immersion baptism—just as the Lord Jesus commanded.

BOOKS BY THE AUTHOR

THE QUESTION ABOUT INFANT BAPTISM: DOES BAPTISM SAVE? - The author was asked by her 5,000-member Lutheran church to write a 12-week Bible course. Discovering her church's baptism of infants is not found in the Bible and Luther's Flip-flop make shocking reading for those who think their baptism saved them.

I WENT TO BAPTIST KID'S CAMP & CAME HOME SPEAKING IN TONGUES : *A Holy Ghost Story* - Can a child's life really be forever changed during one short week at summer church camp? YES! You will be amazed as the author recounts her story of encountering God for the first time at camp as an un-churched child. The seed of salvation began to bear fruit in her life, especially when she realized the funny language she received at the same time was tongues! Can the Holy Spirit really minister to a child before she even knows to ask for His guidance? Read and decide for yourself!

COMING SOON!

"GETTING TO KNOW THE HOLY SPIRIT" – a Study Guide for Individuals and Groups

151

Made in the USA
Middletown, DE
28 December 2022

20119641R00091